*Rose has captured the essence of a powerful force in women's lives—the quest for genuine love. Each biblical profile in this book is a reflection of someone I've met, someone I've counseled, or someone who has nurtured my life. This is an important message for every woman.*

—M. WAYNE BENSON
PRESIDENT, CENTRAL BIBLE COLLEGE
SPRINGFIELD, MO

# WOMAN,
## THOU ART LOVED!

ROSE BELCHER

CREATION
HOUSE
PRESS

WOMAN, THOU ART LOVED! by Rose Belcher
Published by Creation House Press
A part of Strang Communications Company
600 Rinehart Road
Lake Mary, FL 32796
www.creationhouse.com

Unless otherwise noted, all Scripture quotations are
from the New King James Version of the Bible. Copyright
© 1979, 1980, 1982 by Thomas Nelson, Inc. publishers.
Used by permission.

Cover art from award-winning artist
Laura Crane, P.O. Box 430179, Kissimmee, FL 34743,
phone: 407-348-6397

Copyright ©2001 by Rose Belcher
All rights reserved.
Library of Congress Control Number: 2001090581
International Standard Book Number: 0-88419-790-5

01 02 03 04 05   7 6 5 4 3 2 1
*Printed in the United States of America*

# FOREWORD

*I*f women throughout the world were surveyed with the question, *Do you feel loved?*, I fear that the majority of them would answer *No*. And they would have all kinds of reasons for their answer. Some would blame outside influences—parents, children, spouses, fellow-workers, even neighbors. But, from my personal observations, I think that most women would blame themselves. We live in a world filled with pressures and stresses, and most women feel they are in the very center, being pulled in every direction from different people for different reasons.

I will not deny that such circumstances exist, but praise God, there is an answer. And you know what? HE is the answer! No matter what the world hands you, HE is always there—ready and eager to listen, comfort and, if necessary, correct. That's what the love of God is all about.

Throughout the following pages, I want you to see that you're not alone. By turning to some well-known women in the Bible and listening to their personal testimonies, you'll find that these were ordinary individuals who faced many of the same challenges and struggles as women today. But God showed them His love and grace!

So it is with you. As you read, know that God loves you every bit as much as He did these women of the Bible. May He stir your heart so that you know, beyond a shadow of a doubt, *you are loved*!

# PREFACE

hen I began writing this series of stories about women of the Bible, almost a year ago, I had no idea it would become a book. In fact, my first "assignment" from the Lord was to take the life of Ruth and make it into a monologue which could be recited in church circles, especially women's groups. Immediately upon completing Ruth, I was told to do the same with Esther.

It turned out to be so much fun, that I couldn't stop! But, I began to notice that each successive story became less of a "production" and more of a "heart-to-heart" story. My deep desire was and is that women would see themselves in each story and realize just how much God loves them. Times have changed, circumstances have changed—but God hasn't changed! He loves you!

May that thought sink deep into your spirit as you read. May your life be strengthened in the knowledge of His love, no matter what those around you do or say! Woman, thou art loved!

—ROSE BELCHER
SEPTEMBER, 2000

"Praise be to the Lord, who this day has not left you without a kinsman-redeemer...He will renew your life and sustain you in your old age."

—Ruth 4:14–15, NIV

"[Jesus] said to her, 'Woman, you are set free from your infirmity.'"

—Luke 13:12, NIV

"It should be that of your inner self, the unfading beauty of a gentle and quiet spirit, which is of great worth in God's sight."

—1 Peter 3:4, NIV

# CONTENTS

# CHAPTER 1

## *Eve,*

### *a Creation of God*

*I* opened my eyes slowly. How bright it was, and how beautiful! Who am I? Where am I? Where did I come from? Why am I here? I could immediately answer one of those questions, as I hesitantly looked around. Where was I? I was in a breathtakingly beautiful garden. Everywhere I looked I saw lush green bushes, trees and flowers. I was surrounded by perfectly sculpted plots of ground, each with its own special delicacy to eat, to touch, to smell.

I felt a power within me that I instinctively knew

was not my own. And by that same indwelling instinct, I knew that it was my Creator, the One Who had caused me to be in this place. As He encouraged me to stand up and move about, I discovered a pool of clear, sparkling water. As I looked into its depths, I beheld a creature of sorts looking back at me. Its hair was thick and shiny and long. As I moved my head, the creature moved its head also. And when I put out my hand to touch it, the creature did the same thing. I was a bit frightened by it all, until my Creator let me know that He was there with me and that I should have no fear. He explained that this creature was merely a reflection of me. Excitedly I touched my hair, my eyes, my nose, my mouth—and she did the same. I looked down at the rest of my body that the Creator had given me, and it was pleasant to look at.

The Creator then led me a short distance, where I saw another creature lying on the ground in what appeared to be a deep sleep. It looked similar to the reflection in the water, but it definitely was not the same. It was taller, more muscular than I. The features of its face were more chiseled, more powerful looking. The hair was thick and shiny, but shorter than mine. As I looked over the torso, I discovered he was not at all like me. I did not fully comprehend it, but I liked what I saw. Something within me arose and called out to this beautiful creature.

At a slight touch of the Creator's hand, the creature opened his eyes and looked at me. Our eyes locked. Something new and fresh and pure stirred within me.

My entire being called out to him, and I understood immediately that the Creator had made us to be a part of each other, one complete being.

This feeling was confirmed when the Creator introduced me to the man, whom He called Adam. It was no wonder we felt so much a part of each other. I had been created from a part of Adam. The Creator explained that He had created me from Adam's rib for a good reason. Had I come from his head, it would have meant that he was intellectually superior to me; had I come from his feet, I would have been something he could walk upon and crush. But since the rib was a protective covering over the heart, Adam was to be my protective covering, and I would find a permanent niche in his heart.

As the Creator joined our hands, our hearts also were joined, as Adam covenanted with me by stating in a way that set my heart dancing, "This is bone of my bones, and flesh of my flesh; she shall be called woman, for she was taken out of man." Isn't that awesome? Suddenly I felt love pour forth from me. His love filled my being— in much the same way as that of the Creator. He is man; I am woman; we are made by the great Creator, Who spoke forth this beautiful garden and gave it to us as a wedding gift. We are husband and wife. The Creator continued this covenant with, "For this reason a man will leave his father and mother and be united with his wife, and they shall become one flesh."

Adam and I had so much to learn about each other. And we had so much to learn about the lovely garden where Elohim (as we came to know Him) had placed us. Before I was created, Elohim placed only one stipulation upon Adam regarding the parameters of the garden, which he then explained to me. Elohim had warned, "You are free to eat from any tree in the garden, but you must not eat from the tree of the knowledge of good and evil. If you eat of it, you will certainly die!"

That sounded like a simple request. Of all the trees in the garden of Eden, it should be easy to stay away from a single tree. Besides, we were kept busy, enjoying each other and the beauty around us. There was so much to learn, and it was fun to learn it together. Elohim would meet with us at the end of each day, and in excitement, we would explain to Him our adventures of the day. He enjoyed hearing our exclamations over each new-found treasure. We laughed and played and prayed together. The three of us were truly one in spirit and in truth. This perfect world of bliss continued day after day for some time. I don't know for sure how long it went on, but I remember well the day it all ended.

I hesitate to tell you about it because I am ashamed. I don't know why I allowed it to happen. Disbelief in Elohim's words for just a few seconds caused our lives to change forever. I'll try to tell you exactly what happened, with no excuses and no embellishment.

The day began just like any other day. We were filled with joy over each other, happiness with Elohim and expectancy about what new things we would accomplish that day. I don't remember how it happened, but Adam and I went our separate ways for only a short time.

As I was walking alone I found myself heading toward the center of the garden. In the midst of all this beauty, my eyes fastened themselves on the most magnificent tree I had even seen. This was the tree Elohim had warned us about. Its lovely branches seemed to reach out to me, even as its leaves reached up to heaven. And the fruit was so plump and luscious-looking I could hardly believe my eyes.

In the tree's lowest branches sat a beautiful creature. Adam had shown me this creature earlier, explaining that when Elohim granted him the privilege of naming each animal in creation, he had called this one "serpent" because of the extraordinary hissing sounds it made. It was exceptionally attractive. With its glistening skin a myriad of colors, which all blended, it had an almost holy aura about it. I was startled when it spoke—I had never heard any of the other animals speak. I was even more startled at its question to me: "Did Elohim really say that you must not eat from any tree in the garden?"

I knew that to be most untrue and said so immediately. "Oh, no. He didn't say that at all. In fact, He told us that we could eat of any fruit from any of the trees. However, He did say, "You must not eat of the fruit from the tree that is in the middle of the garden; you must not even touch it, or you will die."

The serpent hissed back, "You shall not surely die. You see, Eve, Elohim knows that when you eat of the fruit of this particular tree, your eyes will be opened to knowledge you never dreamed of. In fact, you will be just like Elohim, knowing good and evil. You will be on the same intellectual level as the Almighty Himself! Now, wouldn't you like that, Eve dear?"

To be exactly like the Almighty, the Creator of all that is in existence? What a blessing that would be! Perhaps Adam misunderstood Elohim's directive. Anything that is so desirable to the eye and the mind and the heart must be good. I'll have just one tiny bite; no one will ever know. And with that, I picked the fruit and sank my teeth into its luscious softness, as the juice ran down my chin. The serpent laughed as he scurried down the trunk of the tree and fled as fast as he could. "I must share this with Adam," was all I could think of, as I hurried back to our favorite niche in the garden.

I don't know if I can fully explain, but I *knew* something had happened inside me—body, soul, spirit—and I was not pleased with it. Was it the extraordinary fruit, or was it the fact that I had disobeyed Elohim for the first time? I paid little heed as I rushed back to Adam with the piece of fruit.

He ate, simply because I asked him to. In the twinkling of an eye, our entire world as we had known it changed. Not only had we changed on the inside—our thoughts were no longer pure—but we had changed on the outside too. I looked at Adam; he looked at me. I saw in his eyes not love, but lust. I felt a distrust in him that I had never felt. What had we done? Oh, God, we're so sorry! Can we return the fruit to the tree and pretend it never happened? That's strange—we had never had to pretend anything before. Everything had been good and honest and pure and right. Now there was a darkness within our souls that would never go away. What had we done? Why, oh why, had we done it? The fruit wasn't worth one second of the terror we felt now. Elohim—no, now we must call Him God— what will He say? I know He knows. I know I can never keep anything from Him. He is no longer Companion and Friend; He is God Almighty, our Maker, our Judge.

We had to do something quickly. Adam and I realized for the first time that we were naked. Before, we had the freedom to be what we were created to be and the free- dom to enjoy it to the fullest. Not now. Now we knew we had to cover ourselves; perhaps that would help to cover the shame and regret we felt, both within and without. As we huddled under the fig tree, Adam began plucking the large fig leaves to cover our sinful bodies.

Just as we thought, our Creator knew what we had done. In the cool of the evening, instead of showing our usual excitement and enthusiasm, Adam and I hid. But the Lord God called out, "Where are you?"

Trembling with fear, Adam answered, "I heard you in the garden, and I was afraid because I was naked, so I hid from You!"

"Who told you that you were naked? Have you eaten from the tree that I commanded you not to eat from?"

He knew. And we knew He knew. At this point, Adam reacted in a way I had never seen. He stuttered and cow- ered and said, "It wasn't my fault. The woman You put here with me, she gave me the fruit, and I ate it. It's her fault; it's Your fault; I tell you, it's not my fault."

How dare he put the blame on me! After all, he didn't have to eat. When the Lord God questioned me, I simply answered with truth—at least partial truth, "The serpent deceived me, so I ate."

At this, the Lord God turned to the serpent and said something strange. It was something like, "You will be cursed above all living things; you shall crawl on your belly; you will eat dust." Then came the really strange part: "I will put enmity between you and the woman, between your offspring and hers. He will crush your head, and you will strike His heel."

Who is "He"? What does it all mean? I did not care for His next words to me: "I will increase your pains in childbearing; your desire will be for your husband, and he will rule over you." To Adam He said, "Because you listened to your wife instead of Me, you shall have to toil painfully for your food because the land is now cursed. It will produce thorns and thistles and weeds of every description. Moreover, since you were taken from the ground when I formed you, now you will die and return to the ground from which you came."

And with that pronouncement, the Lord God clothed our naked bodies in animal skins. An innocent animal was forced to give its life so our sins might be covered. To make sure we would never eat of the tree of life and live forever, we were banished from our lovely home. And to ensure our never entering that place again, the Lord God appointed heavenly beings with flaming swords to guard the east gate of the garden of Eden.

With the judgment of the Lord God, we knew that all

mankind would have to pay for our disobedience. I beg you to forgive me for my sinful action. You, too, are paying the price for my sin. However, this promise stirs me with a new-found hope. "He will crush your head" must mean that God Almighty will provide another Adam, who will crush not only the evil of the serpent, but the serpent himself. I await that day with great anticipation. May it come soon, Lord God of all Creation.

*Sarah*

# CHAPTER 2

# Sarah

My name is Sarah. That is not the name I was given at birth, but I'll tell you more about that later. I have had a long, productive life—oh yes, believe me when I tell you, 127 years. I don't look it, but that, too, has its disadvantages, which I'll also tell you about.

My life began in a part of Mesopotamia known as Ur of the Chaldees. I became the wife of Abram, son of Terah, at a young age. To my chagrin and embarrassment, I was found to be barren. I would have done anything to have Abram's child, but the moon-god we worshiped did not allow it.

A short time after the death of my father-in-law, Abram had a strange experience. He was baffled even as he shared it with me. As he was taking a walk alone, he heard a Voice that seemed to come to him from the heavens. The Voice said, "Abram, leave your country and your people and go to the land that I will show you. I will make of you a great nation, and I will bless you. I will make your name great, and you will be a blessing. I will bless those who bless you, and whoever curses you, I will curse. All the peoples on earth will be blessed through you."

At the time he heard the Voice, Abram was 75 years old; I was 65. What was the Voice talking about? What did it mean? We had no idea. We only knew that we must obey. So without questioning, Abram broke his family ties, except for Lot, his nephew, and led us toward a faraway land of which he had never heard.

Throughout the many weeks of traveling, Abram became accustomed to hearing the Voice, which he called "Lord." In fact, as we settled for a short time near Bethel, in the land of Canaan, the Lord appeared to him again, saying, "To your offspring I will give this land." And Abram built an altar there and sacrificed to his new god.

A famine came to the land, so Abram headed toward Egypt, where he planned to stay until the land prospered again. Remember, I was well past my 65th birthday but was told by my peers that I was beautiful. Because of this, Abram gave me instructions upon entering Egypt. "Because you are such a beautiful woman, the Egyptians will kill me to free you to become a wife to one of them. Therefore, you must tell them that you are my sister so they will not harm me." Although I did not understand, I agreed to lie. Because of this lie, I was taken to the king's palace and placed with his concubines, and Abram was treated well. I could have been called into the king's chamber at any time. I was fearful, but I trusted Abram's decision.

It was at this point in time that Abram realized the power of this new god. The Lord inflicted all kinds of serious diseases on both Pharaoh and his household. Pharaoh seemed to know the reason for this awful plague, so he called for Abram. "What are you trying to do to me? Why did you say that Sarai was your sister instead of your wife? What if I had decided to make her my wife? We would have been destroyed by your god!" And with that, he sent all of us, with our vast belongings, on our way. In addition, he gave me an Egyptian maid named Hagar.

We returned to Bethel, where we parted with Lot because of the quarreling among our herdsmen. It was here that the Lord God again told Abram, "Look all around you because every bit of land you can see to the north, the south, the east, the west, all this land I will give to you and your offspring. I will make your offspring like the dust of the earth. If anyone could count the grains of dust, then they could count the number of your offspring. I am giving all of this land to you." And again Abram built an altar and sacrificed to the Lord God.

But I was confused by the Lord God's message. Offspring? I was old; I was barren; I could never have children. So what did He mean by saying that our lives would be filled with children? Although Abram did not understand, yet he believed, I, being more practical, neither understood nor believed.

Ten more years passed. The Lord God had blessed us with great wealth—but no children, which didn't surprise me. Whoever heard of a 75-year-old woman bearing a child? How ridiculous! However, the Lord God had come to Abram again, saying, "To your descendants I give this land from the Nile River in Egypt to the great Euphrates."

Abram believed so fervently that I began to feel guilty, as if it were my fault that no children had been conceived in my womb. One day, as I was thinking about this, I had a remarkable thought. Of course! I would offer Hagar to Abram to take as wife. She was young; she could have many children. And because she was a slave, any children she had would be my property—they would be mine. We could have as many children as we wanted.

When I broached the subject to Abram he hesitated—but only for a moment. He took Hagar into his tent and she became pregnant almost immediately. My plan was working. However, Hagar's attitude began to change drastically. She became vain and proud and looked down upon me, her mistress. She hated me with a passion and daily she would taunt me about my infertility, as her belly grew bigger and bigger.

When I approached Abram with my complaint, he simply shrugged and said, "She's your servant; do with her as you wish." And so I began to mistreat Hagar so unmercifully that she fled from our camp, but only for a short time. She returned saying an angel had appeared to her out on the desert and told her to return to camp. And would you believe the angel supposedly promised Hagar the same thing the Lord God had promised Abram and me, "You will have so many descendants that they will be too numerous to count." Soon after, Hagar had a son whom she called Ishmael.

When Ishmael was 13 years old, the Lord God appeared to Abram, saying, "I am God Almighty; walk before me and be blameless. I will confirm My covenant with you and greatly increase your numbers. You will be the father of many nations." As if that weren't startling enough He added, "You will no longer be called Abram; instead, you will be Abraham, 'father of many nations.' Mine is an everlasting covenant, for you and for all generations to come. I will give you all this land, and I will be your God."

He didn't stop there. He explained that the sign of the covenant would be a ritual called circumcision, where every male child would have a part of his fore-skin removed at 8 days of age. Any male not circum-cised would be cut off from the tribe because the covenant would be broken. The Lord God added further instructions. "Your wife will no longer be called Sarai. Instead she will be called Sarah, 'princess,' for she will bear many generations of royalty."

At this Abraham fell to the floor laughing. "Sarah is 89; I am 99. What you say is an impossibility. You must mean Ishmael, Lord." The Lord God, without hesitation, continued, "By this time next year Sarah will have a son. His name shall be called Isaac, and I will establish My covenant through him. As for Ishmael, I will surely bless him, but he is not the child of My covenant." Abraham arose and immediately called his tribe together. He commanded that every single male should undergo the rite of circumcision, in obedience to the Word of the Lord.

A short time later Abraham was out in the fields when he saw three men approaching. According to custom, the men were invited to rest and eat a meal with him. He quickly ran into my tent and asked me to prepare a feast for these unknown guests. I was happy to oblige.

As I was busily preparing the food, I heard one of the men ask, "Where is your wife, Sarah?" How did he know my name? I had never seen any of them before. Then one of them said, "Within a year your wife will have a son." I tried but I could not stifle my laughter. How absolutely ridiculous—a 90-year-old woman conceiving and bearing a child!

Much to my astonishment, the man asked, "Why did Sarah laugh? Is anything too hard for the Lord? Sarah *will* have a son!" I appeared at my tent door with terror in my heart. I was so afraid that I allowed a lie to escape my lips. "I did not laugh, sir." The man looked at—no, through—me, and I knew Who He was, even before He responded with, "Yes, you did laugh." He was the Lord God Himself.

True to His promise, within a year I conceived and bore a son. We named him Isaac, which means "laughter." You can guess why. God brought laughter to both Abraham and me, and everyone who hears this story will laugh too. Nothing is too hard for our Lord God!

I'm so sorry now that I got ahead of the Lord, a disobedient act that produced Ishmael—a son, but not the child of God's covenant. Even now as I often find Ishmael teasing Isaac without cause, I feel that there will be bad blood between these two brothers, just as surely as there will be an everlasting covenant between God and His people! How can my mistake ever be rectified? Only the Lord God can cover my and Abraham's sin. We willingly offer the firstfruits of our flocks in sacrifice to Him, but that is so temporary. I pray that someday He will provide the right lamb that will take away our sins once and for all.

Miriam

# CHAPTER 3

# Miriam,

## the Prophetess

*I*t all began with the birth of my baby brother, Moses. Little did we realize the effect his birth would have on our nation, both here in Egypt and in the land of promise, which our forefather, Jacob, had left some 400 years ago. Because of the terrible famine in Canaan at that time, Jacob had moved his family of seventy souls, plus his large flock of sheep, to Egypt after becoming reunited with his next-youngest son, Joseph. The story has been told and retold throughout the generations of how Joseph was sold by his ten jealous brothers and ended up in Egypt as a slave in the house of Potiphar. As a result of his being falsely accused he was imprisoned for many years. However, because of his faithfulness, he was greatly blessed by Yahweh and eventually became a ruler in Egypt, second only to the Pharaoh himself. Because of him not only was Egypt saved from a deadly famine, but the many countries surrounding it were allowed to buy food from Egypt because of Joseph's prophetic dreams, which warned them of the impending famine. When the famine ended, Jacob's family was given the beautiful land of Goshen in which to live, and all went well for many years.

Many kings sat on the throne of Egypt during the next 400 years. And the Hebrews grew from a small community of seventy to several million. The Egyptian rulers began to fear our people because of their wealth and influence. And so it was that they were forced into slavery under Rameses I. Still the Hebrews flourished because Yahweh was with them.

It was about this time that I was born. My name is Miriam, daughter of Amram and Jochebed. I had a brother named Aaron. We were Hebrew slaves of the Egyptian crown. As if slavery were not bad enough, an edict was issued that because of the abounding fertility of the Hebrew women, all newborn baby boys would be destroyed at birth. My family was frantic because my mother was pregnant with her third child. I prayed that Yahweh would allow her to birth a healthy baby girl; little did I know that was not His perfect plan.

Soon after, my mother had a beautiful baby boy. The midwife helped us keep the birth a secret for a while. However, by the time he was three months old, we knew it was only a matter of time until a knock on the door would result in our baby being torn from my mother's arms and flung into the Nile River, as had happened to thousands of other Hebrew babies. My mother was worried to distraction as she pleaded before Yahweh every day that He would save her baby.

My mother was a firm believer in Yahweh; her faith was almost unbelievable. And so it was that she awoke one bright, sunny morning and with a smile began some strange preparations. She quickly wove a large basket from bulrushes she had picked on the riverbank. She then pitched it with heavy tar, both inside and out. When it was dry she lined the basket with a soft straw-filled pillow. I was aghast when she called me to her side, cuddling the baby in one arm as she smoothed the pillow with the other hand.

"Miriam," her eyes were sad, but her voice was confident. "Miriam, I have an important job for you. I would trust no one else, not even your father or your brother, to do this. I have begged Yahweh for an answer, and He has given me a solution. You and I will carry this basket down to the river. Everyone will think we are going to wash our clothes. We must not let anyone know we are carrying a baby. I have asked Yahweh to keep the child quiet so no one will suspect anything. The baby will be wrapped all snug and dry; the basket's cover will protect him from the sun. Are you ready?"

I was not at all sure what my mother intended to do, but she was confident it was the right thing—and I trusted her. "Of course, Mother, I'll help you carry the baby down to the river. But what will you do when you get there?"

"Wait, child, just wait and see," she said with a catch in her throat. "Yahweh has told me exactly what to do, blessed be His name. I'll tell you about it as we walk down to the Nile. But remember, no one is to suspect that we are carrying anything other than dirty laundry." She smiled sadly, and we left the house together.

We lived a short distance from the Nile River. Many times Aaron and I had run along its banks until we reached a point where we were forced to stop because it was the outer edge of the royal palace grounds. No one was allowed to enter that area unless he wanted to come face to face with the royal guards. Mother explained her plan as we walked the path leading to the water, then along the water's edge until we came close to the palace compound. The area was surrounded with bulrushes, so we knew we would not be seen.

She gave the baby one last loving pat. Then she looked around quickly before she quietly slipped the basket into the water and gave it a gentle push. She seemed to know exactly where to aim it because it floated away from shore only slightly and headed straight for the cove in front of the palace. It was here that the princess and her ladies-in-waiting came each day to bathe and frolic in the water.

My mother put her hand on my shoulder and smiled. "Do you remember now what you're to do?" I nodded. I couldn't speak because of the huge lump in my throat. She understood. With a quick squeeze, she turned and headed for home. I stood in the midst of a huge clump of bulrushes and waited.

Mother had timed her project well. It was only a short time until I heard the voices of many young girls as they came tripping down the steps that led to the water within the cove. They were laughing and talking and having a good time. How long will it take them to discover my baby brother? And what will they do when they find him? The law of the kingdom said he must be drowned. "Oh, Lord God of Abraham, Isaac and Jacob, hear my prayer and save my baby brother!"

The princess and her maids had played only a little while when one of them noticed the basket, which was inside the cove but nestled against some bulrushes. When they heard a small cry coming from the basket, they all rushed out into the shallow water to retrieve it. They realized immediately that the crying was that of a baby, so they pushed the basket up onto the shore and unfastened the cover. The princess then carefully picked up the small bundle, pulled back the covers and shouted, "It's beautiful! It must belong to one of the Hebrew slaves. In checking him over, she discovered that "it" was a boy, so she knew he was a Hebrew baby.

The princess looked at each of her maids and sternly said, "This is our secret, and I forbid you to tell anyone about it. The gods have directed this child to me, and I intend to keep him. Do you understand?" The girls looked at one another, then smiled at their princess and with lowered eyes, reverently whispered, "Yes, my lady, your secret is safe with us."

I couldn't stand it any longer. I hurried out of my hiding place, hoping they would think I was simply taking a walk along the water's edge. I stood at the edge of the royal property and called out, "Your highness, what a beautiful baby you have. May I make a suggestion? Since so many Hebrew mothers have lost their babies, I'm sure I could find a suitable nurse for your baby, if you would so desire."

She looked at me and smiled. "What a good idea. Please find me a nurse—I want only the best, you know—and bring her here so we can complete the necessary arrangements." I turned and ran as fast as I could back home, where I knew my mother would be waiting.

"Mother, mother, your plan worked! The princess and her ladies discovered the baby, and now she wants to keep him as her very own. And she wants a Hebrew slave woman as a nurse for him. I spoke with her, and she asked that I bring someone immediately. Hurry, mother, hurry with me back to the palace!" All of this exploded from me in one breath as I pulled my mother by the hand in the direction of the river.

My mother let loose of my hand just long enough to kneel, clasp her hands together and send a grateful prayer up to heaven. "Lord God, I praise You that You have answered my prayer. Now direct my steps to know what I should do next to save my baby." With that, we joined hands and headed toward the palace.

To make a long story short, my mother was hired to be the baby's nurse. Since he was pulled from the bulrushes, the princess named my baby brother Moses, which means, "pulled from the water." And so it was that Moses was allowed to stay with us for the first few years of his life. Even after he was taken to the palace to be trained in the ways of royalty, he kept in close touch with us. We were his Hebrew family; the princess was his royal family. Many years passed, but my mother never stopped believing that Yahweh had a special mission for Moses.

By the time Moses was 40 years old, the Hebrew slaves were living an unbearable existence. One day he was out in the field supervising the overseers of the slaves when he saw an Egyptian foreman beat a Hebrew unmercifully for no apparent reason. Unable to control his anger and thinking there was no one else around, he killed the Egyptian. The next day, he was in the fields again when he came upon two Hebrew slaves fighting. When he asked why they were fighting, they answered, "Who are you to judge us? Are you going to kill us as you killed the Egyptian yesterday?"

In a panic, Moses knew his life was in danger, not only from the Egyptian royalty, but from his Hebrew brothers. We did not know the rest of the story until much later because he immediately fled to the southeast country of Midian, where he stayed for forty years. In fact, he married Zipporah, daughter of Jethro the Midianite, and later had a son whom he called

Gershom, which meant, "I am an alien in a foreign land." Moses tried to leave Egypt and the Hebrew slaves behind him, but Yahweh had other plans.

It was a happy surprise to us when Moses reappeared in Goshen, older and wiser. He filled us in on his past forty years. Briefly Yahweh had appeared to Moses as he was tending his flocks back in Midian. I thought perhaps the heat of the desert had gotten to him when he mentioned that an angel of the Lord appeared to him out of a bush that burned ferociously but was not consumed. It was when he was examining the bush that the Lord God spoke to him of many things. One I remember was that he was to remove his sandals because the place on which he was standing was holy ground. But even more amazing, the Lord told him that he was chosen to free the Hebrew people from Egyptian slavery. He was to lead them back to the Promised Land, which they had left some 430 years before. He was given instructions as to how it should be done, which he didn't share with us. However, he did say Aaron and I were to be an important part of the exodus plan.

As you might expect, the Pharaoh was not pleased when Moses presented himself and demanded that the Hebrew people be freed. The Lord caused plagues to come and curse the land because the Pharaoh refused to free them. After each plague (they included the waters being changed to blood, then frogs, gnats and flies, then sickness to the livestock, then boils upon the people, followed by hail, locusts and complete darkness over the land), the Pharaoh would concede—and then change his mind when the plague was lifted. The strange part was that all these things happened to the Egyptians, but not to any of the Hebrews.

However, just before the tenth plague appeared, the Hebrews were given specific instructions that were to be followed each year as a memorial. Each family was to prepare a pure and spotless lamb for sacrifice. The blood of that lamb was to be painted around the lintels and doorposts of each house. When the death angel passed over the entire land of Egypt, only those houses where blood had been applied were passed over; in each of the other homes, the firstborn was killed. A feast was to be prepared, where the lamb must be completely consumed and where only unleavened bread was to be eaten. We were to prepare ourselves for a quick exit out of the country. We packed what few necessities we thought we would need and followed the plan just as the Lord had given it to Moses.

When the Pharaoh found his firstborn dead, he demanded that the Hebrews leave the country. We hurriedly took our belongings, much of it the treasures given to us by the Egyptian people who urged us to leave for their safety. We were barely out of the city when the Pharaoh realized what he had done. He immediately called for what was left of his armed chariots and sent them after us.

By that time we had gotten as far as the Red Sea. On the other side was freedom. But how could we ever cross that large body of water? We knelt as a body of one and pleaded Yahweh's mercy upon us. About that time, we looked behind us to see Pharaoh's army fast approaching. Moses, who had been praying to the Lord for guidance, then did something I shall never forget. He raised his staff aloft and shouted to the petrified people, "Stand firm, and you will see the deliverance the Lord will bring you today. The Lord will fight for you; you need only to be still." Then he stretched his hand out over the water and drove the sea back by a strong east wind. The sea parted, and there was a wide path of dry land for us to walk across, with a wall of water to our left and to our right. The Lord had said He would deliver us this day, and He had kept His promise!

Pharaoh's army was drawing closer, so we wasted no time is getting ourselves over on the east side of the Red Sea. With a possible two million men, women and children, it could have taken us far more time than we had, but somehow Yahweh moved us quickly and, at the same time, slowed down the royal chariots. He is truly a God of miracles! But that's not all. Just as the last of our people were almost across, the royal army was about to enter on the far side of what had been the water's edge. As they reached the midpoint, suddenly the walls of water came crashing down, and the river flowed south as it always had done, carrying the men, horses and chariots to their instant death. We were free at last!

After resting awhile, Moses gathered the people for a service of worship and praise to Yahweh. I could not contain myself; I gathered many of the women in the assembly, and we led the congregation in a dance of praise unto the Lord. Yahweh gave me these words to go along with the music and dancing:

> I will sing unto the Lord,
> For He hath triumphed gloriously,
> The horse and rider thrown into the sea!
> The Lord, my God, my Strength and Song
> Has now become my victory!
> He has become my Salvation!
> I will prepare Him a habitation;
> My father's God, and I will exalt Him!

And then in grateful worship, directly to Him, we sang:

> Who is like unto Thee,
> O, Lord among the gods?
> Who is like unto Thee: Glorious in holiness,
> Fearful in praises; doing wonders...
> Who is like unto Thee?

Wouldn't you think we would have been full of worship and praise for the rest of our days for the miraculous workings of the Lord? And yet three days later we arrived at a desert oasis, where the water was bitter and could not be drunk. We immediately tagged the place "Marah" for its bitterness. And then we began to complain to Moses and Aaron.

At once Moses went to the Lord in prayer. The Lord showed him a tree, which when he cast it into the water, the water became sweet and pure. At that time, Yahweh made a promise to us: "If you will do right and heed the commandments of the Lord, I will put none of these diseases upon you that I put upon the Egyptians, for I am the Lord who healeth thee." How sorry we were for our complaining. The Lord was with us; all we had to do was live according to His commandments.

But we failed miserably, time after time after time. And because of our disobedience the Lord put a curse on all those more than 20 years old. None of us, including Moses, would be allowed to enter into the Promised Land. The exceptions were Joshua and Caleb, who followed the Lord obediently in spite of the rest of the tribesmen. Therefore, the Lord was going to make us wander in that part of the land known as the Fertile Crescent until all of the adults had died. And during all those years, neither our clothes nor the sandals on our feet wore out.

Even with this terrible sentence, Yahweh provided for our needs. There were many examples. For instance, we had begun to complain about the food— or lack of it. (How easy it was to forget the horrible life we had been forced to live for hundreds of years.) "Moses, you have brought us out of Egypt only to kill us with hunger in the wilderness."

Moses again went before the Lord with our complaints. And the answer came. "Behold, I will rain down bread from heaven for you to eat. It will fall fresh on the ground every morning, and you shall pick only enough for your household. If you take more than you need, it will rot before your eyes, and the odor will be overpowering. Each evening I will provide fresh meat for you to eat. By these acts, you will know that I am the Lord your God."

And provide He did. Because we did not know what it was we were gathering, we called the bread "manna." It was similar to coriander seed; it was white, and it tasted like honey wafers. We were asked by the Lord to take up a pot of the manna and put it inside the Ark of the Covenant as a sign to future generations that the Lord did provide for the needs of His people.

In another experience, I am ashamed to admit how wrong I was. Without any warning to us, Moses married an Ethiopian woman. Although it was none of our business, Aaron and I became angry with our brother for this awful thing he had done. We went to Moses with our complaint. After he talked with the Lord, the three of us were called into the Tabernacle, where the Lord spoke directly to us. To our question, "Are we not also prophets, the same as Moses?" the Lord answered, "If there is a prophet among you, I will make it known unto him in a vision and a dream. But Moses is different. I will speak to him mouth to mouth, and he shall be more like Me than any other man." In other words, "How dare you speak against My anointed one?" A cloud appeared over the Tabernacle, and as it lifted I could not believe my eyes. In those few minutes I had become a leper. My body was covered with while blotches of dead skin and open sores. I would soon be dead.

I knew that I was unclean, so I hurried to my tent. Aaron stayed behind to plead with Moses for my life.

He acknowledged that we had foolishly sinned against our leader and therefore against Yahweh Himself. Again, with great compassion, Moses went before the Lord. "Heal my sister now, O God, I beseech Thee." Yahweh heard and answered, "She shall be made whole, but she must be shut out of the camp for seven days. After that, she shall be received into the congregation again." And so I was sent outside the camp, and in seven days my body was made whole again. Praise the name of the most high God, who heals all our diseases and forgives all our sins!

We are now in Kadesh, and I am old. The Lord has told us that we shall not see the Promised Land. I am sorry for my sinful ways, but I know the Lord has forgiven me. However, I have also learned that even when our sins are forgiven and forgotten, we must sometimes bear the consequences of those sins. Because of my disobedience, I will not see the land of promise. But the Lord Jehovah has assured me that because I am forgiven I will rest in the bosom of Abraham when I die. I praise Him for His goodness and His everlasting mercy, both now and in all the generations to come. He is my God, and I trust Him completely. Blessed be His holy name!

Rahab

# CHAPTER 4

# Rahab

### of Jericho

Greetings! I come to you in the name of the Lord God of the Hebrews. However, it was not always so, but that's why I'm here. I want to tell you what happened to me as a result of my listening (and not even knowing that I was listening) to the voice of the Lord God. Even as He saved me, He can save you—but I'm getting ahead of my story.

My name is Rahab, and I come from the city just west of the Jordan River called Jericho, the city of palms. It was a beautiful city in the land of Canaan back in the days after what you believers call the Exodus. The great leader, Moses, had led the Hebrew people for forty years before he died and was replaced by Joshua. It was Joshua's responsibility to lead the people into the unknown land that the Lord God had promised them hundreds of years before through Father Abraham.

I was known by other names, not quite as pretty as Rahab. The most complimentary one was "innkeeper." And I was, in a way. In a more modern vernacular, you would call me a "madam." Other names more closely tied to me were "harlot" and "prostitute." I tell you this not because I'm proud of my past, but to show you how much the Lord God loved me, in spite of my sinful lifestyle.

My home was built on the city wall, which gave me access to all the comings and goings of the city. This was why I was called into the presence of the king of Jericho and asked to help capture two Hebrew spies who had entered the city. Little did the king know that I already had been approached by these men just days before. For some reason, which I didn't understand until much later, I listened to their pleas and hid them in the upper loft of my home. Of course, I couldn't tell the king what I had done, so I stretched the truth a bit. "Yes," I complied, "I saw the men a few days ago. Perhaps, O king, they left the city just before the gates were closed. Perhaps your men can overtake them if they leave immediately. The king followed my advice, and I hurried home to see that my spy friends were safe. They had cleverly hidden among the stalks of flax that I had stored, just in case the king's men had been told of their whereabouts.

"I know this is your land that the Lord God has given you," I said, after I assured them that they were safe. "We in Jericho are deathly afraid of you because we have heard how the waters of the Red Sea were dried up so your people could escape from Egyptian bondage. We also heard about your destroying King Sihon of Heshbon and King Og of Bashan because they would not allow the Hebrews to pass through their land. Every man, woman and child were destroyed in more than the sixty high-walled cities that were captured. Your God is powerful; He is the God of the heaven above and the earth beneath. Now because I have shown you kindness, you must swear you will show kindness to my mother and father, brothers and sisters, and deliver them from death that is likely to come."

The spies replied, "After the Lord gives us this land as He swore He would, we promise to deal kindly with you and yours. Because you have saved our lives, we will save yours."

I didn't know if I should believe them or not. After all, they were the enemy. They decided it was time for them to return to the Hebrew camp, so I helped them escape over the city wall by providing a rope for them to slide down to the outside. I explained what I had told the king about their having escaped from my house. "Now it would be wise for you to go to the mountains and hide for three days. By that time the king's men will have returned to Jericho, and you will be safe."

As they agreed, the spies gave me a piece of scarlet cord, which I was to hang from the window through which they escaped. As they bade me goodbye, they warned, "Be sure to bring your parents and siblings into your home, and we will guarantee their safety. However, if they are found outside your house, we cannot be responsible for them. And if you decide to turn us in, our promise for your safety will be revoked by the Lord." With that they were gone.

A short time later my wall-side view let me know that something was about to happen. Thousands of young Hebrews had made their way toward Jericho. I emphasize "young" because, except for the two leaders, Joshua and Caleb, all the people were less than twenty years old. They had been forced to stay in the wilderness for forty years until all the adults had died of old age. The story was that they had disobeyed the Lord God, so He had punished them by not allowing them into the "promised land" of Canaan. Our citizens were terrified, not only because of the young people— who knows what they had in mind—but because of the large number of them. We went neither in nor out of the city because of our fear of the unknown. All I could think of was, "Will the spies keep their promise if and when they take over our city?"

From the conversations outside the wall, I learned that their army was composed of some 40,000 men. They were instructed to lead a procession, followed by seven Hebrew priests, each blowing a ramshorn.

Following them would be a beautifully carved pure gold box, which was constructed with poles on either side so it could be carried on the shoulders of four priests. No one was allowed to touch the box, called the Ark of the Covenant, because the Hebrews had been taught that this signified the presence of the Lord God.

Each day for six days this procession marched around the wall of the entire city in silence, except for the priests blowing their trumpets. What were they doing? And why? What was their strategy? With each passing day the people of Jericho became more terrified.

I awoke early on the seventh day to the sound of muffled marching feet. It was barely dawn. Something different was going on today, and we could feel the heightened pressure from outside the wall. The entire entourage marched around the walls as they had done the previous six days. However, this time they did not stop, but continued a second time, then a third, then a fourth, fifth, sixth. By this time Jericho residents were in a panic, but there was nothing they could do. They didn't understand what was going on, but they knew it was not good.

The seventh encirclement was completed. For a few minutes there was silence. Then the priests blew their trumpets powerfully. Joshua, the Hebrew leader, cried out in a loud voice, "Shout, for the Lord has given you the city!" With that command, all the people outside the walls shouted at the top of their lungs, and the walls of our city crumpled to the ground.

I don't like to think about what happened next because the entire city became a blood bath, as the citizens were killed. I was almost surprised when a group of soldiers entered my house, not with weapons of destruction, but with instructions that everyone in my house was to be taken to safety. The men had kept their promise. We were saved!

What a powerful God those Hebrews worship! I want to follow Him too. I want Him to take my life and use it for His glory. Perhaps He will use me to become a part of His faithful line of history in the eons to come. Because of my one small act of compassion, He has picked me up from a sinful past and has planted my feet in His footsteps, from which I shall never depart. Bless the Lord, O my soul! And all that is within me, bless His holy name!

Deborah

# CHAPTER 5

# *Deborah,*

## *the Judge*

*B*lessed are You, oh Yahweh!
You alone are God—
    The God of Father Abraham,
    Isaac and Jacob.
    You alone are King of Israel.
    Israel needs no king but you.
    When the princes of Israel take the lead,
    When the people willingly offer themselves,
        Praise the Lord!

Hear this, you kings; listen you rulers—
I will sing to the Lord, I will sing,
   I will make music to the Lord,
   To the God of Israel!

   In the days of Jael, the roads were unsafe,
   Travelers took to winding paths,
   Village life in Israel ceased—
   Ceased until I, Deborah, arose,
   Arose as a mother of Israel.

   When they chose new gods,
   War came to the city gates,
   And not a shield or a spear was seen
   among 40,000 in Israel.

   My heart is with Israel's princes,
   With the willingness among the people.
   Praise the Lord!

   The people of the Lord
   Went down to the city gates—
   "Wake up, wake up, Deborah!
   Wake up, break out in song!
   Arise, oh Barak, take captive your
      captives, oh son of Abinoam."

   Most blessed of women be Jael, The wife
      of Heber the Kenite.
   Most blessed of tent-dwelling women.
   Sisera asked for water; she gave him milk.
   Her hand reached for the tent peg,
   Her right hand for the workman's hammer;
   She struck Sisera, she crushed his head,

She shattered and pierced his temple,
At her feet he sank, he fell,
There he lay—dead.

Through the window peered Sisera's mother;
Behind her lattice she cried out,
"Why is his chariot so long in coming?
Why is the clatter of his horses delayed?"
The wisest of her ladies answer her—
Indeed, she keeps saying to herself,
"Are they not finding, dividing the spoils:
A girl or two to each man;
Colorful garments for my neck—
All this as plunder!"

Our God is an awesome God, a God of victory! By my song, you must have guessed that I am Deborah, prophetess of the tribe of Ephraim and wife of Lappidoth.

I was content in each of these positions because both helped me to know and understand that I was in the will of Yahweh, Who guided my life day by day. Little did I know, as I sat under the palm tree each day settling disputes among the townsmen, that Yahweh had a bigger job for me.

First He told me to send for Barak of the tribe of Naphtali and command him to assimilate an army of 10,000 men from both Naphtali and Zebulun and take them to Mount Tabor. There Yahweh promised to deliver Sisera, commander of the enemy troops, into Israeli hands.

Barak was a man of war; he should have been over-whelmed with pride that Yahweh would choose him to rout the enemy of his people. Instead, either because he didn't believe me or because he was afraid, Barak refused to do as the Lord commanded unless I went with him. I hesitated for an instant until I felt the Spirit of the Lord urging me to agree. However, the Lord was not pleased with Barak, and I relayed this message to him. "I agree to accompany you to the Kishon with your 10,000 men, but the honor that was intended for you will go, instead, to a woman."

Barak was satisfied with the arrangement. I was not so confident. After all, I was only a woman in a man's world. What business did I have leading an army against the enemy of our souls? The Lord comforted my spirit, and I knew I was in the right place at the right time. The land of Canaan had overrun us so many times because we had refused to obey the Word of the Lord. For many generations since Joshua, the people had done evil in the sight of the Lord, and each time, Yahweh had punished them by delivering them into the hands of their enemies. Each time, the people had cried out to God, Who would send a messenger to judge them and bring them back into His good graces. Some of the better-known judges of the past included Othniel, brother of Caleb, and Ehud, the left-handed Benjamite who slew the king of Moab by hiding a sword under the right side of his tunic.

Israel enjoyed peace for eighty years after overcom-ing Moab. However, the people again turned their backs on God until He sold them into the hands of King Jabin, whose commanding officer was named Sisera. They had oppressed Israel for more than twenty years. As in many previous times, Israel cried out to God, and He heard and answered them. That's where I, a newly anointed judge, became the leader of an army that, under the banner of Yahweh Nissi, brought Sisera to his death and Canaan to her knees.

This is how it happened. Sisera thought he was wise when he led his chariots and men into the Jezreel Valley on the Kishon River. He could attack the weak Israelis from any point he wished. Sisera did not know, nor did he understand the power of Almighty God. On the appointed day, our 10,000 men advanced down Mount Tabor and wiped out the entire enemy army. Sisera was the only one left unharmed. In his fright, he fled on foot to the "friendly" Kenites, to the tent of Jael.

Jael met him at the door and invited him into her tent. Because no man except a woman's husband could enter her tent, Sisera reasoned that this would be an ideal hiding place from the Israeli army. But Jael had a plan. Graciously, she offered her guest a bed so he could rest. When he requested a glass of water to quench his thirst, she honored him with a glass of refreshing goat's milk instead. She covered him and immediately he fell into a deep sleep.

It was at that point that Jael picked up a tent peg and hammer and quietly drove the tent peg through his temple, killing him instantly. When Barak arrived in pursuit of Sisera, Jael showed him what she had done. Canaan had been defeated under the leadership of Yahweh and his obedient servant, Deborah.

I feel compassion for the mother of Sisera. With their 900 iron chariots, the Canaanite army felt sure of victory. But instead of a victory celebration, which she had prepared for her illustrious warrior son, she was forced to prepare a dirge for his burial. Instead of beautifully embroidered garments brought home as plunder, she was to wear the drab garb of mourning for a son who should have been the victor. However, when Yahweh is the Leader, no army can outwit Him—not even one with 900 iron chariots. Our God is a mighty God!

That's why you find me here, praising the Lord for His great victory over our enemies. Now I complete my song to Him:

> So many of Your enemies perish, Oh Lord!
> But may they who love you be like the sun
> When it rises in its strength!
> Praise the Lord!

And the land of Israel had peace for another forty years.

Ruth

# CHAPTER 6

# *Ruth,*

## *the Moabitess*

*S*halom! I'm not a Jew in the strictest sense, but my roots go back to Lot, the nephew of Father Abraham. My name is Ruth. I am a Moabitess—that is, I was born in the small country of Moab, on the eastern side of the Dead Sea. My bloodline of the past is not half as important as my future bloodline. The Lord God of Israel has made me a promise concerning my son, Obed, and our future generations. Let me tell you a story that, if I didn't know it to be true, I would think it was a fairy tale.

It all began several years ago in Moab. When I became old enough to marry, I was given to Chilion, one of the two sons of Elimelech, the Jew. Elimelech had come to Moab from Bethlehem when his boys were small because of the great famine in Judea that lasted for many years. The family had settled down in Moab when suddenly Elimelech died. Naomi, his wife, was left to raise her sons alone. It was hard for her. But it wasn't long before she was her pleasant self again. (Her name means "pleasant.")

My Chilion had a brother named Mahlon. He, too, married a Moabitess, who happened to be my best friend. Her name was Orpah. We married about the same time, and we did many things together. We were a well-known foursome in our small town. And we loved to include Mother Naomi because she was so much fun to be with. We loved her. We were about to celebrate our tenth wedding anniversary. How fast the years had flown! Our one regret was that we had had no children. Orpah and Mahlon also were childless. Except for this, our lives had been very happy.

And then tragedy struck again. Without warning both Chilion and Mahlon died of a peculiar disease about which our doctors knew nothing. It happened so quickly. All three of us women were in shock for some time. Because of all the things Naomi had taught us about her wonderful Jehovah God, we had come to believe in Him too. And although we didn't understand why He would allow Chilion and Mahlon to be taken from us, we felt confident that that same Jehovah God had not and would not forsake us. However, we saw a change come over Naomi. It was just as if she had given up her faith. Her husband and now her two sons had been taken from her. It was almost more than she could bear. We couldn't get her out of her deep depression.

It was with great joy, then, when Mother Naomi came home from the marketplace some time later and gave us the news. The land of Judah had finally come through its years of famine, and the economy was looking good again. Naomi wanted to return to her beloved Bethlehem. She told us this news with a tiny bit of hope and joy in her voice—something we hadn't seen in a long time. Suddenly she looked at us, and the tears began to roll down her tired, old face. "Girls, you must both return to your parents' homes where they can take care of you. Our Jewish law says that upon the death of one's husband, the next brother of the dead man should marry the widow so children can be produced. I have no sons, and I am old and will never bear more sons. Besides, even if that were possible, you wouldn't want to wait around for 20 years for them to grow up and become your husbands. Therefore, you have my permission to become a part of your birth parents' household again." With that, Naomi kissed each of us and bade us goodbye.

With a long hug, Orpah kissed Naomi, packed her belongings and headed in the direction of her parents' home. I watched as her parting figure grew smaller and smaller. Then I looked at Mother Naomi. I love them both so much! What should I do—stay here and continue my deep friendship with Orpah? We had so much in common, from the background of our growing up years to the past ten years, when we were wives of two of the greatest men Jehovah God had ever created.

Or should I break every tie that bound me to the only country I had ever known and head into a new country, whose language and customs I knew nothing about? I would be with my beloved Naomi. Her country would become my country, her people my people, and, of course, her God my God. I wanted to take care of her for the rest of her life. And then when she died I wanted to be buried where she was buried.

It was a hard decision to make, and although Naomi tried to talk me out of it, I knew it was the right one. Judea would become my new country; Bethlehem would become my new hometown. So we packed our few treasured belongings and headed toward faraway Bethlehem. The journey took several weeks. As we came nearer to my new homeland, I could feel an excitement and anticipation like I had never felt before. What did Jehovah God have planned for us? What did He have in mind for me? I had put myself into His hands, and I was at peace.

That was not so for Naomi. It wasn't that she had lost her faith or her desire to live. I think she was feeling a bit sorry for herself, and she wanted the people in her old hometown to feel some of the pain she was feeling. We entered into the gates of the small city, and several old friends were there to greet her with, "Can this possibly be our Naomi?" To that she, almost childlike, retorted, "Don't call me Naomi, the pleasant one. Instead call me Mara, for Jehovah has dealt bitterly with me." I was a bit embarrassed, but I think they understood how she felt. They gave her loving pats as we made our way to the little home she and Father Elimelech had left many years before.

The house was small but adequate for our needs. There was a good piece of land too, but it had lain barren for years. And now it was the beginning of the barley harvest. We needed food, and I had promised to take care of Naomi, so I asked the whereabouts of the best barley fields, where I could work and provide food for our needs.

It was then that Naomi spoke of a kinsman of her husband who lived in our area. His name was Boaz, and he was wealthy. In fact, he owned much of the grain that was now being harvested. I pleaded and Naomi gave me permission to go to the fields of Boaz and glean the grain after the reapers had finished. You see, the Jewish law provided for the needy by allowing them to harvest any leftover grain in the field. Naomi and I had no money, so we fit into that category. However, one could hear all kinds of tales about how the gleaners were mistreated, especially the young women. Many times they were sexually violated simply because they had no one to protect them. Before I left the house Naomi and I prayed that Jehovah would guide and guard my path. His blessings are new every morning, and He proved it far beyond my wildest dreams.

When I arrived at the field of Boaz bright and early the next morning, I was surprised to see so many other gleaners already at work. The morning flew by as we walked behind the reapers to gather the grain that was left behind. By high noon, my back was aching from the continuous bending and stooping. And the sun became very hot.

I took out but a few minutes to rest when I noticed a handsome gentleman, who was obviously an important personage, come into the field and talk to some of his reapers. Their response to him indicated beyond a shadow of a doubt that he was the boss. I felt their eyes upon me, and the next thing I knew, Lord Boaz, whose name I had picked up from the other gleaners, was standing in front of me. Without introducing himself, his first words were, "You are more than welcome to glean my fields. Please do not place yourself in danger by going to any of the nearby fields. My men have orders to protect you and your reputation. When you become thirsty, my men have been instructed to allow you to drink from the company water vessels."

I flung myself on the ground before him. Gleaners were never treated so kindly, so generously. Why me? When I found my voice and could control myself, I asked, and he answered, "News in a small town travels fast. I know all about your leaving your country; I know of your devotion to your mother-in-law since the death of your husband. You left your old life behind and you willingly followed a brand new, unknown way of life. The Lord God will bless you abundantly for your putting your trust completely in Him. Allow me to invite you to share the noon-time meal with my reapers and me."

Without hesitation the reapers shared their food with me. It tasted so good. Naomi and I had not allowed ourselves to eat so abundantly, and I could hardly wait to take my treasure of grain home and share the good news with her. That afternoon and for many weeks to follow, I gathered enough food to feed Naomi and me for at least a year.

As you may or may not know, harvesting grain requires tasks be done in a certain order. After reaping, the sheaves of grain are brought to the threshing floor to be winnowed. The wheat is separated from the chaff, which is blown away. When the harvest reaches its peak, the workers are put into shifts. Some work in the fields by day; others winnow the grain throughout the night. If they weren't winnowing, someone had to be there to protect the crop from thieves. I said all that to explain why, on a beautiful fall day, Mother Naomi came to me with an idea that probably had been churning within her for weeks.

"Ruth, my dear," she said, her eyes brimming with love, "it's time you put an end to your mourning for Chilion. He would want you to know peace and security and happiness once again. Therefore, I want you to bathe, put on your best dress and perfume, and go to the threshing floor tonight. Boaz will be there all night to guard his grain while the reapers get some much-needed rest."

A tremor of guilt ran through my body. How did Naomi know of the attraction I felt toward Boaz and had felt for weeks? How did she know we had shared many of our lunch times together, where we had learned so much about each other? She continued with a most preposterous plan. I blushed as she explained to me step by step what I was to do. I was to go to the threshing floor but not make myself known to Boaz. Then after he had eaten his late meal and had lain down on his mat to sleep, I was to uncover his feet and lie down at the foot of his mat. She said that Boaz would instruct me further.

What Naomi was doing was very much in keeping with the Jewish law of kinsman-redeemer. Since I was a Moabite, Naomi probably thought me ignorant of this law. What she didn't know was that Boaz had explained this law explicitly during one of our lunchtime conversations. It was evident that he had a purpose for telling me about it. It was as if he wanted it to sink into my very being before he told me more. With my heart dancing for joy, I quietly assured Mother Naomi I would do as she said.

It was near midnight before Boaz retired to his mat for the night. I had been hiding in the shadows for hours, it seemed. It took but a short time for him to fall into a deep sleep. I approached his bed quietly and lay down as Naomi had directed. I was about to fall asleep when something startled Boaz out of his sleep. It could not have been I; I had been as quiet as a mouse. I hoped it was the angels of Jehovah God. Once he was awakened he knew he was not alone and called out in the darkness, "Who's there?"

Very respectfully, very nervously, I made my presence known. I hesitated only slightly as I answered: "I am Ruth. Since you are my kinsman-redeemer, please spread a corner of your garment over me." In reality I was proposing to him. I waited with bated breath for what seemed like hours. It was probably one minute. I could tell something was causing him to hesitate. Maybe he didn't want to marry me. Perhaps I had made a fool of myself by obeying Naomi.

He sat up in the dark and tenderly took my hand. "It is true that I am a kinsman, but dear Ruth, there is one other person who is more closely related to you than I. Let me speak to him tomorrow. If he wants you, that is his right and privilege." I shuddered at the thought of becoming anyone's wife but Boaz's. He continued, "But if he is not willing to take on this responsibility, I will be more than happy to."

He bade me to lie at his feet for the rest of the night. However, to prevent unwanted gossip, I arose before daybreak and hurried back to Naomi—though not before Boaz had given me a large bag of fresh, clean grain to take with me and a tender smile that told me exactly how he wanted the decision to go.

I did not hear this part of the story until later, but here's what happened. Later that same morning Boaz went to the city gate, knowing his kinsman would come along. He had with him the required ten elders to make the proceedings legal. He explained to—I'll call him Levi, although no one ever mentioned his name—that Naomi was back in Bethlehem and intended to sell her land. Since Levi was next of kin he had first rights to buying that land. Levi agreed to buy it. Then Boaz exposed the hidden agenda—me. "If you buy the land you realize, of course, that the widow Ruth is a part of the deal because the property must be kept in her dead husband's name."

Boaz is so smart. He knew the kinsman would not accept the entire package. Instead he answered, "I don't want my life to change, Boaz. I have my own self to consider. As the next in line, I plead with you to get me out of this legal responsibility."

As Boaz told me later, he made a big to-do by frowning and saying, "If you won't take the responsibility, then I guess I'll have to." Then he immediately announced to the elders and the people gathered that he had "acquired the widow Ruth and her property." Then he hurried to tell me what had happened. We were both so happy! And, of course, Naomi was pleased that her well-laid plans had succeeded. We were married immediately in a beautiful ceremony.

We have now been married more than a year, and you can see how Jehovah has blessed us with a baby boy that I hold in my arms! It has been prophesied that our little Obed will become the father of many great men in the coming generations. But right now I just want to love him and enjoy him and bless the Holy God of Israel for all His benefits!

# Hannah

# CHAPTER 7

# Hannah

*G*reetings to you! My name is Hannah. May I tell you what the Lord has done for me? I hope your heart is as full as mine as I relate to you a marvelous true story of a compassionate God who keeps His promises.

My husband is Elkanah of Ephraim. As was the custom of our day, I am one of two wives of Elkanah. Peninnah, the first wife, was blessed with many children, while I, the second but most beloved wife, was barren. I loved children, and I wanted them more than anything in the world, but for some reason the Lord had not so blessed me.

Our temple of worship was on Mount Shiloh, where Eli and his two sons, Hophni and Phinehas, were priests. Our religion required that we travel to Shiloh at least once a year to offer our sacrifices to the Lord God. While Elkanah would give small portions of his sacrifice to Peninnah and their children, to show his love for me, he always gave me a double portion for my sacrifice. I greatly appreciated this act, but my heart was breaking because of my barrenness.

And Peninnah didn't help the situation because she continually berated me with cruel taunts about my inability to conceive.

It was time for Elkanah to take his family with him to Shiloh for the yearly sacrifice. After we arrived I was so hurt and depressed that I broke into tears before my husband. He looked at me helplessly, as he cried, "Hannah, oh Hannah, why are you weeping? Why are you so sad? Why don't you eat? Don't I mean more to you than ten sons?"

Since he didn't know what else to do he gently took me by the arm and led me to the temple gate, where Eli was sitting. A short distance away was the altar, and I made my way to it and fell down, sobbing uncontrollably. Bitterly, as I silently prayed to the Lord, I made a vow to Him. "Oh, Lord Almighty, look upon my misery and remember me. If You will give me a son, I will give him back to You to serve you for the rest of his life."

Not being able to hear me, but seeing my lips move,

Eli evidently thought I was drunk. He haughtily approached me with, "How long will you continue your drinking habit? Get rid of your wine."

Shocked at his rebuttal, I quickly dried my tears and sobbed, "Oh, not so, my lord. I am a woman who is greatly troubled. I have not been drinking; I have been pouring out my soul to the Lord, in great anguish and grief."

Somewhat ashamed, Eli stepped back and, hanging his head in remorse, said, "Go, my daughter, go in peace, and may the God of Israel grant you your petition."

With that blessing racing in my heart and mind, I left the altar area, received some food and felt a real peace in my spirit for the first time in years. I began to feel that the Lord had heard my prayer this time. Perhaps He would even answer it. I went back home to Ramah feeling that a great burden had been lifted.

Would you believe, in less than one year after returning from Shiloh, I conceived and bore a son? I named him Samuel, which means "heard of God." I loved him and nurtured him with all my being throughout his babyhood.

He had just reached his third birthday when it was time for the yearly trek to Shiloh. I had not gone since before Samuel was born. But this time I knew I had to go. It was time for me to give the greatest sacrifice of my life—my son! I had to keep my promise to the Lord. So I packed his clothes, and taking a bull, some flour and a skin of wine for my offering to the Lord, I accompanied Elkanah and Samuel to Shiloh.

As we approached the temple gate, I timidly approached Eli because I thought he might not recognize me. "I am the woman who stood before you four years ago and prayed to the Lord for a child. I promised Him that if He would grant my petition, I would return the child to Him as soon as he was weaned. The Lord has granted my request, so now I must keep my promise. I now give him over to your care. The rest of his life will be dedicated to doing the Lord's work."

With a heart that was breaking but a spirit that was rejoicing, I knelt again at that same altar, and I prayed, aloud this time:

> My heart rejoices in the Lord;
> In the Lord my horn is lifted high.
> My mouth boasts over my enemies,
> For I delight in Your deliverance.
>
> There is no one holy like the Lord;
> There is no one besides You;
> There is no Rock like our God!
>
> Do not keep talking so proudly,
> Or let your mouth speak such arrogance,
> For the Lord is a God who knows,
> And by Him deeds are weighed.
>
> The bows of the warriors are broken,
> But those who stumble are armed with strength;
> Those who were full hire themselves out for food,

But those who were hungry hunger no more.
She who was barren has borne seven children,
But she who has had many sons pines away.

The Lord brings death and makes alive;
He brings down to the grave and raises up.
The Lord sends poverty and wealth;
He humbles and He exalts.

He raises the poor from the dust,
And lifts the needy from the ash heap;
He seats them with princes,
And has them inherit a throne of honor.

For the foundations of the earth are the Lord's;
Upon them He has set the world.
He will guard the feet of His saints,
But the wicked will be silenced in darkness.

It is not by strength that one prevails;
Those who oppose the Lord will be shattered.
He will thunder against them from heaven;
The Lord will judge the ends of the earth!
He will give strength to His King,
And exalt the horn of His anointed!

And so we went back to Ramah empty-handed but full of joy. I am already making plans for my yearly visit with my son. Each year I will make him a new robe and take it to him at the temple sacrifice.

The Lord has promised to bless me with more children—three sons and two daughters—and I believe Him! But my son Samuel will always be special, a miraculous gift from the Lord. And he will continue to grow in stature and in favor with God and man. Thank You, Lord God Jehovah, for Your lovingkindness to Your people!

Queen Esther

# CHAPTER 8

# Queen Esther

Happy Purim!

Purim is the annual feast day when my people celebrate their deliverance from King Xerxes of Persia. It
happened a few years ago, when I was much younger
and more naive. But it is celebrated every year with
great jubilation and merriment.

It all began after Jerusalem fell and the Jewish people were carried into Babylonian captivity for seventy
years, just as the prophet Jeremiah had predicted.
Toward the end of this period, Cyrus, the king of

Persia, defeated the Babylonians and allowed the temple in Jerusalem to be rebuilt. Shortly thereafter Cyrus was followed by Xerxes, who ruled from his royal throne in the city of Susa.

It was in the third year of Xerxes' reign that news came that Xerxes' queen, Vashti, had refused to present herself to the king as he had requested. Everyone knows that you do not refuse the king anything. He is all-powerful, and to do so labeled you a criminal. Such a crime necessitated her being deposed and a new queen chosen to replace her. A countrywide search was conducted, and many beautiful young virgins were brought into the royal harem at Susa. Before she was ever presented to the king, twelve months of beauty treatments were prescribed for each girl who won his royal favor. At the end of this preparation time each girl would be taken to the palace, where she would spend one night with the king. She would not be called again unless the king was pleased with her and summoned her to himself by name.

My name is Esther, blood cousin and adopted daughter of Mordecai, high-ranking civil servant of the king. Unbeknownst to them of my Jewish blood (Mordecai had warned me not to tell anyone), I was one of those chosen for the king's harem. I had gone through a year of being pampered and massaged and perfumed in preparation for my being called into the king's chambers. That day finally came. Much to my surprise and delight, the king was pleased with me—so much so that he immediately made me his new queen.

What an honor! I determined that I would do everything I could to become the best queen of all time.

One day soon after my crowning Mordecai came to me with word that there was a conspiracy to assassinate my husband. I immediately passed this dreadful news on to Xerxes, telling him its source. As a result the would-be assassins were captured and hanged. And so life continued peacefully in the king's palace for four years. The king was pleased with me, and I honored him at every opportunity.

At this point in time Haman, the Amalekite, was elevated to a high position in the king's court. Let me remind you that the Jews and the Amalekites had been enemies for 500 years, since the days of King Saul, the Benjamite. Since Mordecai was a Benjamite, he refused to honor Haman by bowing down to him, as had been commanded by the king. When the royal officials told Haman of Mordecai's refusal, they also passed on the news that Mordecai had confessed openly to being a Jew. Haman was enraged. He began to look for a way to annihilate not only Mordecai but every Jew throughout the kingdom.

His first step toward this end was to cast the "pur," or lot, to find out the best time to carry through this dastardly deed. The casting was done, and the date selected was eleven months from that date. That much time was needed because the Jews were scattered widely throughout the royal provinces. King Xerxes agreed to allow Haman to do as he pleased with the Jewish people in his country. Of course, he had no idea that would include me because he still did not know my religious heritage. A copy of the royal edict was issued to every province. Every Jew would be killed and the hatred between them and the Amalekites stilled forever.

I heard about all of this when news came to the palace that Mordecai was outside the palace gate, mourning with other Jews, in sackcloth and ashes. I wanted to know what was going on. A copy of the official edict was brought to me. As I stared in horror, the royal guards gave me Mordecai's personal request. I was to go before the king and plead for the life of my people. I sent a quick reply to Mordecai, reminding him that anyone who approached the king's court without a royal invitation was subject to instant death. The only exception to this law was for the king to extend to the uninvited his golden scepter. I loved my husband, and he loved me, but the law was the law.

Mordecai answered my plea with harshness. His message said, "Don't ever think that because you are in the palace that you alone of all Jews will escape. As you stated, 'The law is the law.' You are not exempt from it."

I was terrified. I could not take the chance. On the other hand, my life was in as much danger as any other Jew in the province. What should I do? After much thought I received an answer from on high. I sent a note by messenger to Mordecai, stating, "I will do as you ask. But you must first gather all Jews within our city and fast for me. Do not eat or drink for three days and nights. My maids and I will do the same. At the end of three days, I will approach the king, even

though it is against the law. And if I perish, I perish."
Is it any wonder that I shook with fear? This decision
could mean my death, but not doing anything would
also mean my death and the death of all my people.

The next three days passed quickly. On the fourth
day, after abstaining from all food and drink, I felt I
had made the right decision. I dressed more carefully
than usual. The silken robes I put on were the king's
favorites. My hair was dressed in his favorite style. I
must do everything in my power to be so attractive for
him that he would forgive my forwardness and extend
to me his golden scepter of acceptance. I approached
his throne with some reluctance, lowering my eyes in
honor to him. As I did so, he extended his golden
scepter to me. He was willing to accept my uninvited
presence! He smiled as he took my hands in his. "My
queen," he said, "what is your request? I will give you
anything up to half my kingdom, if you so desire it."

My heart was jumping for joy, as I took a small step
forward. "I have but a single request, my king," as I
looked him in the eye. "My request is simply that the
king and Haman would come today to a banquet that I
have prepared." He agreed instantly. So both came to
my royal quarters to partake of the feast I had prepared.

After the royal meal, as they sat drinking their wine,
the king again asked me this question: "My queen,
what is your petition? Anything up to half my kingdom
will be granted." I smiled gently and said, "Oh, king, I
ask only that the king and Haman come to my royal
quarters again tomorrow for a second banquet, which I

will prepare for you. At that time, I will answer your question."

Later the king told me that he returned to his quarters but could not sleep. So he called for the records of the kingdom to be read to him. In the reading he found the record of Mordecai's exposing his would-be assassins some time earlier. He could hardly believe it when he was told that no honor or recognition had been given to Mordecai for his loyalty to his king.

Haman was standing outside the king's chambers. He was called in and asked a simple question by the king. "What should be done for a man whom the king would like to honor?" Haman drew himself up straight and tall. His entire demeanor said, "Who would the king wish to honor except me?" He answered, "For that man I would order a royal robe that the king has worn and put him on a horse that the king has ridden. And a royal crest should be placed on his head. After that, let the honored man be led through the city streets by one of the royal princes, proclaiming as he goes, 'This is what is done for the man whom the king wishes to honor.'"

The king was jubilant. "Haman, that is a striking idea! Go at once, get the robe and horse and crest as you said and present it to Mordecai the Jew, who sits at the king's gate at this moment." Of course, Haman had to obey the king, so he did as he had suggested.

Zeresh, Haman's wife, later told me the outcome after he left the king's presence. When he rushed home, Haman covered his head in grief. At about that time the king's eunuchs arrived to bring him to my royal quarters for the second banquet I had prepared.

After the sumptuous meal, they were drinking their wine when again Xerxes asked me, "My queen, what is your petition? You know that I will grant you up to half my kingdom." This was the moment I had been waiting for. This was the fork in the road that would lead to the destruction of my people or a complete pardon. Carefully I began to speak in almost a whisper, "Oh, king, I have but one request. Spare my people! I am a Jewess, and recently my people have been threatened with total annihilation." When the king demanded to know who the adversary was, I quietly pointed, "The enemy is this vile Haman."

Haman slunk to his knees on the floor, even as the king left the room in a rage. He then crawled over to my couch where I was reclined and fell on top of me— just as the king re-entered the room. The king became livid! "Would Haman dare to molest the queen even as we are all together in the same house?" he screamed. One of the king's eunuchs then came forward with the news that Haman had just completed a 75-foot gallows, which he had prepared for Mordecai's death. Without hesitation the angry king bellowed, "Hang Haman on it!" And it was done.

As a love gift, Xerxes gave me all of Haman's estate. He then removed his signet ring and gave it to Mordecai. I appointed Mordecai to oversee my new estate. The king then issued another decree that freed every Jew in the nation. Not only were they freed as a people, they were legally given the right to defend themselves against any possible enemy. Every city, every province celebrated with feasting and dancing. The Jews agreed to make this event a national day of celebration forever, to be called Purim, for the casting of lots to plot the destruction of the Jewish people.

I am grateful that I was able to be used to bring freedom to my people. Certainly the Creator had put me in the right place for such a time as this! Bless His holy name!

# CHAPTER 9

# *"That Woman" of Sychar*

*I*t's disgusting, that's what it is. It's degrading. "That woman"—don't they know I'm a human being, just as they are? "That woman" makes me feel like less than a person— which is exactly what those who know about me want. I might just as well be a leper; that would give them a proper excuse for steering clear of me. It's none of their business how or with whom I live. They, with their small-town, puritanical ideas! I'll stay away from them if they'll stay away from me!

Let me introduce myself. I am not "that woman"; I

am Shoshana of Sychar. You'll recognize Sychar as the age-old town in Samaria where our forefather Joseph was buried upon the return of the Hebrews from Egypt hundreds of years ago. Sychar is also known for having the sweetest, purest water in Samaria. When Father Jacob (whose sons became the leaders of the twelve tribes of Israel) lived in this area, he dug a well. To this day, it is known as Jacob's Well. It is so deep that when a pebble is thrown into its opening, many seconds pass before one hears a splash from down below. And the water is the coolest, clearest, most refreshing liquid you could ever put to your lips.

Jacob's Well is on the edge of town, which means it is used not only by the townspeople, but is a cheerful welcome to weary travelers coming to and from Judea to the south and Galilee to the north. However, those travelers do not include the holier-than-thou Jew. I am a Jew, but only partly so. Long ago when our nation was captured by the Assyrians, my forefathers were taken captive. Over a long period of time, intermarriage with the foreigners made us what the "true" Jew calls a "half-breed." To them we are a desecration of the Covenant between the Jew and his God. So much so were we an abomination that righteous, blue-blood Jews would not even cross our land to get to and from lower and upper Israel. To do so would cause them to become "unclean." You'd think it was our fault that we had become captives of the enemy.

Because we were not allowed to worship Jehovah in

Jerusalem, we had done the next best thing. We had set up our worship center at Mount Gerazim, which gave the true Jew something else to hold against us. There is no love lost between our Jewish brothers and us Samaritans. Neither is there a friendly feeling between my Samaritan neighbors and me. Because of my "impure" reputation—I make no apologies for it; life is rough, and you do what you have to do to survive—I was snubbed by the women of Sychar. Each evening they loved to gather at the well and catch up on the day's news events. It was a daily hen-clucking party. I was not a welcomed member of this group of socially pure ladies. In fact, had I approached them, they probably would have picked up some of the large, smooth stones surrounding the well and thrown them with the intention of killing me. So I was forced to fill my water vessels in the heat of the day when no one else came near the well. It makes no difference to me; they're just jealous because I am attractive and attracted to the opposite sex. I could tell them some stories that would curl their tightly bound hair. Variety is the spice of life, right? And I like mine spicy.

On a particularly hot day I was headed toward the well, my empty water jug perched on my shoulder, thinking about a new man in my life. He had moved in a short time before, so I couldn't tell yet if he were husband material. Heaven knows I had had enough husbands, I should be able to judge between the good and the bad—if there was such a thing. Play it cool for a while, give him what he wants, and take from him all you can get. That's my motto. It works for me. Ask any of those snobbish townswomen. They'd give anything for my kind of life, but they'd never admit it. Sure, I have pangs of loneliness. Sure, I'd like to be respected. But no one I know can fill that hungry hole in my heart.

It was with these churning thoughts that I made my way to the well. To my surprise there was a good-looking young man sitting on the well's ledge. I couldn't believe my eyes. He was a Jew. He must be disoriented, or he'd never step foot on our land. It was apparent that he didn't know who I was because he smiled. There was something about him that made me feel like a person of worth. I had never seen anyone like him.

In spite of his relaxed friendliness, he looked tired. He must have been traveling for hours, and it was now high noon. The tiny bit of shade provided by the well would not shelter him for long. I hesitated, not sure how I should react to this stranger, when he spoke. "Woman, would you please give me a drink of water?"

I reacted stupidly; I said the first thing that popped into my head: "You are a Jew, and I am a Samaritan. Jews do not associate with Samaritans. How can you ask me for a drink?"

He gave me the strangest answer, "If you knew the gift of God and Who it is that asks you for a drink, you would have asked Him and He would have given you living water."

What in the world is this man talking about? He must be suffering from heatstroke. I'd offer him some water, but he has no container from which to drink. Perhaps I should just go along with him so he won't get too agitated. "Sir, you have nothing to draw with, and the well is deep. Where can you get this 'living water'?" Let's see just how learned this Jew is... "Are you greater than our father Jacob, who gave us the well and drank from it himself, as did his sons and flock and herds?"

Without hesitation, he gave a strange reply. "Everyone who drinks this water will be thirsty again. But whoever drinks the water that I give him will never thirst. Indeed the water I give him will become in him a spring of water welling up to eternal life."

I didn't understand his strange words, but they flooded my entire being with hope. Is this what I've been looking for all my life? "Sir," I said, "give me this water so I won't get thirsty and have to keep coming here to draw water."

His reply set me back. "Go call your husband and then come back." An unaccustomed redness flooded my face. I had to be honest with this peculiar man. "I have no husband," I said as I hung my head. How would he react? Would he get up and leave? Would he know what I really was? He quickly said, "You are right when you say you have no husband." How did he know? He continued, "The fact is, you have had five husbands, and the man you now have is not your husband. What you have said is true."

This man must be a prophet. He knows my past. Let's change the subject fast. If he is a prophet, he'll also know Jewish history. Let me try this. "Sir, I see that you are a prophet. Now, our fathers worshiped on this

Mount Gerazim, but you Jews claim that the proper place to worship is in Jerusalem. What do you think?"

His answer startled me because I didn't understand all he was saying. I knew this man had something I needed. So I listened intently as he spoke. "Believe me, Woman, a time is coming when you will worship the Father neither on this mountain nor in Jerusalem. You Samaritans worship what you do not know; we Jews worship what we do know, for salvation is from the Jews. Yet a time is coming, and has now come, when the true worshipers will worship the Father in spirit and truth, for they are the kind of worshipers the Father seeks. God is Spirit, and His worshipers must worship in spirit and in truth."

What is this man saying? He speaks of the past, but also of the future. I think he's talking about the coming Messiah. "I know that Messiah is coming. And when He comes, He will explain everything to us." Now that should settle him down. He stood and looked into my eyes. "I who speak to you am He!"

I was speechless. He claims to be the Messiah. And I believe that He is. But if that were true I could not stand in His presence. My sinful lifestyle rose up to face me headlong for the first time in my life. I must change my way of living. And with that thought upper-most in my mind, I dropped my water jar and ran all the way back into Sychar. I no longer cared what the townsmen thought of me. I had a story to tell them, and tell them I must! I felt clean inside, and I knew the old life was forever behind me. The Messiah would know my heart. Surely He could change the people of Sychar, even as He had changed me! Perhaps they'll listen to my story.

I saw a large group of townspeople standing together. I quickly approached them before they had a chance to scatter. "Come, see a Man who told me everything I ever did. Could this be the Christ?"

Not only did they listen to me, they made their way immediately to the edge of town and Jacob's Well. After speaking a short time to us, we knew beyond a shadow of doubt that this Man was truly the promised Messiah! We had so much to learn. The Christ/man who called Himself Jesus ben Joseph promised to stay with us and teach us about this new way of life to which each of us was committed. We had to know more about this living water. As they later told me, "We no longer believe just because of what you told us. Now we have heard for ourselves, and we know this Man really is the Savior of the world!"

Needless to say, my name is now different. Instead of "That woman," I am now called "Shoshana, that woman who told us about the Christ." To Him belongs all the glory! Thank You, Master!

*Mary*
*of Bethany*

# CHAPTER 10

## Mary of Bethany

y name is Mary, and I live in Bethany with my sister Martha and brother Lazarus. I would love to tell you about what has happened to our household since Jesus became an important part of our lives.

It all began when an important Pharisee from Bethany known as Simon the Leper, a close friend of ours, decided to honor Lazarus by giving him a birthday dinner. Jesus was an invited guest. We had known Jesus for about three years. We had listened to His teachings and seen His many miracles, so we knew He was a special person—the promised Messiah, we believed. I loved to sit at His feet and absorb His very presence into my spirit.

I loved His simple stories that explained His mission on earth. However, I didn't fully understand His continued warning about His coming death and resurrection. In fact, it frightened me. He said that was why He came into the world—so all who believed He was the only begotten of Jehovah would have their sins forgiven and live with Him forever in heaven. I didn't know much about this heaven He talked about, but it couldn't be any better than being able to sit at His feet and listen to His expounding on every subject that was a part of our lives. Jesus knew about my past, which had been very sinful until I had allowed Jesus to become my Lord. He continually assured me of His love and forgiveness.

And so when we were invited to Simon's, I made a decision to do something that others might feel was foolish. But I felt in my heart that it had to be done, even though I didn't understand why. Stored in my hope chest was an alabaster jar containing about a pint of nard. It was given to me when I entered adulthood, possibly for a dowry to my future husband since its value was about a year's wages. I carefully took the jar from its wrappings and hid it in the folds of my gown as I headed down the street to Simon's home.

By the time I arrived, the guests had been seated and the meal had just begun. I picked out Jesus from the crowd and boldly walked straight toward him. The tears began to flow uncontrollably, and my heart was exploding with love, as I broke the lovely jar and poured it over His feet. Kneeling before Him, I unbound my thick mass of hair and gently wiped His feet, as the heavenly fragrance of the nard filled the room.

The silence I had caused by my appearance quickly turned into mayhem. Everyone began speaking at once. The disciples were disturbed. Even Simon spoke in a demeaning way, "If this Jesus were a real prophet, He'd know what kind of a woman is touching Him; she is a sinner!" Even this did not bother me because I was in the holy presence of the Lord, and nothing else mattered except that I continue worshiping Him.

I could barely hear Jesus as He explained, "Simon, I have a story to tell you. Listen closely and tell me what you think. Once upon a time, there were two men who owed money to a lender. One owed 500 denarii; one owed 50. However, neither man could repay the amount he owed, so the lender canceled the debt of both of them. Now, Simon, which of these men do you suppose will love the lender more?" Simon, a bit red-faced, answered reluctantly, "Well, I suppose the one who had the bigger debt canceled."

With a twinkle in His eye, Jesus said, "Simon, you have judged correctly." Then in a more serious tone, He looked from Simon to me and continued, "Do you see this woman? I came into your home, and you did not give Me water for My feet. But she has wet My feet with her tears and wiped them with her hair. You did not give Me a traditional kiss, but she has not stopped kissing My feet. You did not pour oil on My head, but she has poured perfume on My feet. Therefore, Simon, I tell you that her many sins have been forgiven for she loved much." He looked straight into Simon's eyes and said, "But he who has been forgiven little loves little." With that Jesus helped me up and bade me go in peace. He was pleased with my offering. Oh, how I loved Him!

That's why it was so difficult for me a short time later, when Lazarus became ill and we knew he would die if Jesus did not come heal him. We sent servants up north to where Jesus was teaching and informed Him of our need, but He didn't seem too concerned, according to our messengers. We watched and waited, but to no avail. Lazarus died, and we could do nothing. He was immediately placed in our family tomb, and our mourning began.

When we heard Jesus was entering our town, Martha went out to meet Him. I stayed home because I was somewhat put out by Jesus' response to our pleas for help. Martha told me later that His answer to her statement that had He been in Bethany, Lazarus would not have died was, "Your brother will rise again."

How ridiculous! Of course we knew Lazarus would rise because we believed in the resurrection of the body at the end of time. But now he was dead, and no one could deny it. Jesus' reply was, "I am the resurrection and the life. He who believes in Me will never die. Now where is Mary? I want to see her."

A bit reluctantly I came out to meet Him. With tears flowing down my face, I fell at His feet and said, "If

You had been here, Lord, my brother would not have died." Jesus looked at me with compassion, and He wept. Then He asked, "Where have you laid him? "

We approached the tomb, and Jesus ordered that the opening stone be removed. We were appalled. Lazarus had been dead for four days. The odor would be unbearable. Jesus simply said, "Did I not tell you that if you believed, you would see the glory of God? "

The stone was removed. Jesus came closer to the opening. Then He turned His eyes heavenward and said, "Father, I thank You that You have heard Me. I know that You always hear Me, but I say this for the benefit of those standing behind Me, that they may believe You sent Me." Then He cried loudly, "Lazarus, come forth!"

We waited with bated breath. Time stood still. And then from the blackness of the opening, Lazarus moved with difficulty into the bright sunlight. We stood like statues for several minutes. Finally the reality of what had just happened took root. Our brother had been raised from the dead! He was alive again! We stood there wondering what to do next. In His practical way Jesus quietly said, "Remove his grave clothes and let him go." He made this miraculous act seem so simple. Our Lazarus was alive because of Him. We would never forget this day as long as we lived.

Time has passed. Just as Jesus had taught, He was crucified, but not unlike Lazarus, in three days, He arose from the dead! We are now free from our sins! Hallelujah! And He has ascended to the Father, where

He has promised to prepare a place for us when we die. I can hardly wait to see Him again; what a celebration there will be! Join me there, won't you please?

Mary Magdalene

# CHAPTER 11

# Mary Magdalene

My name is Mary. My hometown is up in the Galilee area of Magdala. That's why I'm called Mary the Magdalene, or Mary Magdalene for short.

Magdala is several days' trip from here on the Mount of Olives, just east of Jerusalem. What am I doing so far from home? At this point, I'm not sure. Events of the past couple of months have happened so quickly, and I understand little of what is going on.

But perhaps talking about it will help clarify my thinking. My head is spinning, and I don't know where to begin, but I'll try to tell you everything that has happened. Just be warned, you might find much of it hard to believe, but upon my honor as a Jewish woman, everything I say is true.

Hmm. My honor. That would have been a joke three years ago. You would not have recognized me then. You see, I had battled all my adult life with darkness. My mind was dark with confusion and evil thoughts. My body was tortured with darkness, as I sold myself to anyone who would have me. My mouth spewed forth venom at anyone who crossed me; I would become so angry I could have killed with no thought of remorse. My heart was dark, and so often I simply wanted to kill myself to get away from the darkness. But I never succeeded. Those times when I came close to death, I could feel stirrings within me urging me to end it all. This would be followed by a horrible, inhuman laughter that caused people to think me insane. My outward appearance matched the inner darkness of my soul. Bathing, keeping my hair clean and bound was of no importance to me. If people thought I was bad and ugly, I'd show them just how bad and ugly—and dirty—I could be.

I don't look or act like that now. What changed me? The most wonderful man came into my life. No, no, no...not that kind of relationship. I had had plenty of those, and they never brought satisfaction and peace. This man brought me that and more. Have you heard of Jesus, the Messiah? Briefly, He is the Son of God. He is the fulfillment of all that the prophets told us about in the sacred Scriptures. I came to know Him soon after He began His ministry. At 30 years old, He was baptized by the prophet John at the Jordan River. John had introduced Him to the crowd as "the Lamb of God, who takes away the sins of the world." John's words had spread far and wide, even to Magdala. These words would not let loose of me. I knew I was a sinner, but I didn't know how to get rid of my sins. They were far bigger, far stronger than I was.

Jesus had returned to Galilee to begin His preaching by choosing twelve men who believed that He was the Messiah—at least part of the time. Gradually, persistently, He taught them the things of God, whom He always called "Father." They became known as His "disciples," and they seldom left His side.

It was one of those times that Jesus had traveled around the northern end of the Galilee and entered Magdala. Something inside me was scared to death of Him, and I tried to run away from His penetrating gaze. However, He took my dirty hands in His, wiped the grime from my face, and looked me straight in the eyes and rebuked the devil from me. I had no idea what was going on. I only knew I wanted to be set free. The "things," the "beings" inside me left me one by one, with screaming and howling and vile, contemptible words. But they had to leave. And I felt them leave—seven in all. I felt like a newborn baby, clean and fresh and filled with gratitude and love for the One who had set me free. I became a part of His ministry from that day.

I was among the throng that gathered on the east side of Galilee when the Master—He had become my Lord and Master—visited the country of the Gadarenes. Outside the city he met a man who everyone said had been possessed by demons for years. He refused to live in his family's house; he lived among the tombs of the dead instead. He refused to wear clothing and when he was bound by chains to keep him from hurting himself, he broke them as if they were sewing thread.

When the Master asked his name, the wild man answered, "Legion, for we are many." Jesus looked about Him and saw a herd of pigs on the hillside overlooking the eastern shore of Galilee. He quietly commanded the demons to leave the man and enter into the pigs. Almost instantly, the maddened animals ran violently down the hillside and directly into the sea and were drowned. Many in the crowd were frightened and left, but I was not one of them. I had been in the same position as the demon-possessed man. A couple of years ago, I would have acted much like he did. I knew how that man felt. So I wasn't surprised when we turned around and saw him, clothed and sane, sitting at the feet of the Master. I knew his life would be changed as mine had been.

Jesus had allowed me to become a part of His ministry team, and I thought that's what would happen to the Gadarene. But instead Jesus told him to return to his hometown and tell everyone what had happened to him. Of course, it wouldn't take a lot of words because the townspeople knew all about him. In fact, they had been afraid of him. His entire being was now so changed, they couldn't help but see that he had been miraculously healed. It was no surprise that the next time we were in the area, the people of Gadara welcomed us with open arms. They told me of the change that had taken place in their town because of this man's testimony. Most of the townspeople had become believers.

There were so many miraculous healings in the Capernaum area because the people were so on fire as a result of the Master. Jairus' daughter had died, and Jesus brought her back to life. And a woman who had been hemorrhaging for more than twelve years touched the hem of His garment in the midst of a huge crowd and was instantly healed. There were hundreds of miracles like these, day after day after day. And yet few were healed in Jesus' hometown of Nazareth because the people did not believe that Jesus was the Messiah, God's Son, sent to redeem God's people.

Jesus was a great teacher. He told us many beautiful, meaningful stories that were so simple because they touched us right where we lived. One I especially remember was about a farmer who went out to his field and planted seeds. Some of the seeds fell by the wayside and were either trodden down or birds ate them. Some fell on a rock and then withered because there was no moisture. Some seeds fell but were choked because of the thorns that surrounded them. Then there were seeds that fell on good ground that grew and bore fruit one hundred-fold.

We didn't understand all He was saying, so we asked Him. He answered us in a strange way that I've been pondering ever since. He said, "To you, My disciples, is given the knowledge of the mysteries of the Kingdom of God, but to others I give parables that they neither see nor understand." Then He went on to explain the story of the farmer. "The seed," He said, "was the Word of God. Those by the wayside hear the Word, but the devil comes and takes it away. Those on the rock hear the Word with joy, but they have no roots, so when temptation comes, they fall. The thorns are those who hear and then go forth but are choked by the cares and pleasures of this life and are unable to bear fruit at the time of harvest. Those on good ground hear the Word of God and obey it. And they bring forth abundant fruit." I want to produce abundant fruit, don't you?

Jesus became well-known to the people of Galilee, Judea and Samaria.

One day Jesus and His men left Jerusalem and headed toward Galilee. Jesus headed straight for Shechem, a Samaritan city, where Jacob's Well was located. The well was more than 1,750 years old but still produced the cleanest, purest water in the land. Jesus was weary and thirsty from His long journey. It was noon so there would be little, if any, traffic around the well. So He decided to stop and rest while the disciples went into town to buy lunch.

He had just gotten comfortably seated when a woman approached the well to draw water. I knew this woman from my past life. Her name was Shoshana*, but she was better known as Shani. She and I had been in the same "social" group before Jesus entered my life

---

* This is the same Shoshana who told her story in chapter 9, "*That Woman* of Sychar"; however, this is a retelling of her story from Mary Magdalene's perspective.

and made me a new creation. My values had changed, so our paths had ceased to cross. She told me the following story later.

It was unusual for anyone to draw water at this hour of the day because of the noonday sun. Most women would come during the early morning hours or the cooler hours of the evening. Those who came at noon would have to be there because they did not associate with the "normal" townswomen. It was a pretty good guess that she was either a leper or a woman of ill repute. Since she was not covered as a leper would be to hide her rotting skin, she had to be a "bad" woman, one whom the other women in town would call a tramp while the men would hungrily ogle her as she passed by.

So you can imagine Shani's surprise when the Master asked her for a drink of water. Slowly letting the water bucket down into the 130-foot well, she hesitatingly remarked, without looking directly at Him, "How can you, a Jew, ask me, a Samaritan, for a drink? Jews do not even speak to Samaritans." Quietly, Jesus looked her in the eye and said, "If you only knew who it was who asked you for a drink, you would have turned it around and asked Him, and He would have given you *living* water." This baffled her, but when she questioned Him, He answered, "Whoever drinks of this water will thirst again. But whoever drinks of the water I give shall never thirst because it will become a fountain springing up into everlasting life."

Shani had no idea what His words were about, but suddenly she knew that whatever this water was, she wanted it. She didn't want the humiliation of having to draw water for her needs during the hottest part of the day. He evidently had an answer that she knew nothing about.

The Master then made a strange request. "Go, get your husband and come back here to the well." Shani's face paled and then colored deeply. Although she had been married several times, the man she was living with was not her legal husband. Much to her surprise, this embarrassed her. She didn't know why, but for the first time in her adult life, she felt ashamed. So rather than trying to explain her situation, she simply answered, "Oh, I don't have a husband." That seemed like an honest enough answer that should satisfy the Jewish traveler.

He shocked her with His soft but outspoken retort, "Yes, you're right, you don't have a husband. However, you have had five husbands in the past." How did He know that? "And the man with whom you're living is not your husband." How did He know so much about her? The only answer within reason was that He was a prophet of Jehovah. No one outside Shechem knew that much about her, and the citizens of the town were not about to broadcast the activities of this woman who put a blot on their city's moral character.

Then the prophet began speaking of "the Father" and how He was seeking true worshipers who would worship Him in spirit and in truth. Shani knew this man must be referring to the coming Messiah. She had been taught about Him when she was growing up. She had tossed it aside as she became an adult because she had earned the right to do her own thing, be her own person. Trying to impress Him with her spiritual intellect, she drew herself up and repeated the catechism she had learned as a child. "Oh, yes, I know the Messiah is coming. And when He comes, He will reveal all things to us." Looking her squarely in the eyes, He said gently, "I am He."

It's a good thing the disciples reappeared at this point because she was at a loss for words. She didn't bother retrieving her waterpot; she had to get away from that Man who claimed to be the Messiah. But in the time that it took to get back to the city, she felt a change taking place inside her. Gradually, she knew His words were true—He was the Messiah! She believed Him beyond a shadow of a doubt. She had to tell someone the good news! They had to experience what she had just experienced!

She knew she couldn't tell the women of Shechem what she had learned. They would turn their backs on her and go on their way as if she never existed. As she neared the city, the usual group of men was at the gate, talking over the news of the day and arguing in a friendly manner. Not stopping to think of their reaction she ran to them and breathlessly announced: "Come, come to the well and meet the man who told me all kinds of things about my past. Could this be the Messiah, for whom we have waited so long?"

Every man there moved as a unit and marched toward the well. They had no idea why. It was as if they were being pulled by a huge magnet. They were compelled to go see the man. The men not only listened to the Master; they believed and accepted Him as their Messiah, the Savior of the world. What a happy city Shechem was, as for two days its citizens celebrated their new birth!

That was typical of the way the Master worked. Quiet, gentle, to the point. When He spoke, it was as if you and He were alone and He was looking into the depths of your soul. There was nothing that could be hidden from Him.

I suppose that's what bothered the church leaders in Jerusalem. They didn't understand Him because they didn't want to understand Him. The cost was too great. They could not do His bidding and "rise up and follow" Him. So they went about finding ways that they might be rid of the "rabble-rouser," as they called Him. With their money and power, it didn't take long to instill fear in the hearts of the people about this far-too-popular heretic of the Jewish law.

In fact, it was one of His closest companions who planted the kiss of betrayal, which led to His arrest in the Garden of Gethsemane on the eve of Passover. Judas Iscariot, one of the twelve disciples, led the mob, who in turn bound Jesus and led Him to the house of the high priest Caiaphas. Thinking it would be to their advantage to have the Romans convict Him, they led Him to Pontius Pilate. However, Pilate could see no fault in Him, so he sent Him to Herod, who happened to be in Jerusalem at the time. Herod berated Him, mocked Him and arrayed Him in a gorgeous royal robe, but fear caused him to return the "criminal" to Pilate. Pilate thought he could appease the crowd by having the criminal flogged and then released. However, the mob demanded crucifixion, even going so far as to say, "His blood be upon our heads and the heads of our children."

It was reported that another one of the twelve, Simon Peter, denied that he even knew Jesus, let alone that he had lived in the company of the Man for more than three years.

Jesus was beaten unmercifully; a crown of thorns was pressed down upon his head; and He was forced to carry His own cross to the hillside outside of Jerusalem called Calvary. Most of His followers fled after His arrest. Only a few of us followed Him down the crowded, cobbled street, through the Damascus Gate to Golgotha, the place of the skull, where criminals were raised up on crosses, their hands and feet impaled with large nails, as they died a slow, agonizing death.

I walked beside Mary, Jesus' mother, as we trudged the path to that place where her Son would give His life. It was only then that we recalled—and understood—what He had been telling us for more than three years. He was the Son of God. We believed that. But we thought His Kingdom would be an earthly one, with the crumbling of the Roman Caesar, the fall of Pilate and the disgrace of Herod. The believers were supposed to reign with King Jesus, who would rule the world in peace.

But now, more dead than alive, we watched while He was nailed to the cross like a common criminal at 9 A.M. on the sacred day of Passover. Not until the hours passed and the noonday sun had turned dark, and a great earthquake struck, did we realize that this Man, our Lord and Master, was the real Passover Lamb— sacrificed to take away the sins of the world! He had told us time and again, but we simply didn't under- stand until it was too late.

It was almost sundown, the beginning of the Sabbath, when Jesus drew His last breath and it was finished. Two old friends, Nicodemus and Joseph of Arimathea, had received permission from Pilate to take the body of Jesus from the cross and lay it in Joseph's brand new tomb. What a sad day Passover Sabbath would be! I helped Mary, weak and broken, back to her home, along with John, who had promised Jesus he would take care of her as if she were his own mother. I promised her that we Marys and Salome would get up early on the first day of the week and go to the tomb, where we would prepare Jesus for a proper burial.

The Sabbath dragged by, as did our grieving bodies. What we thought would become a heaven on earth had become a living hell. How could we ever go on with- out Him? He was our Life, our Breath, our All in All! It was almost too difficult for us to follow the Master's words of, "Father, forgive them for they know not what they do."

Sunday morning finally came. There had been all kinds of rumors about the soldiers being posted at the sealed tomb so the disciples would not steal Him away. Some even believed that Jesus would be raised from the dead, as He had raised Lazarus of Bethany. I was too heartbroken to think or feel. I wanted to die. Had it not been for my desire to help Mary, I don't know what I might have done.

Long before sunup Mary, Salome and I were on our way to the tomb carrying packets of sweet spices with which to anoint the Master's body. As we walked we discussed whom we could find to roll away the heavy stone from the opening of the tomb. "Perhaps the soldiers are still there. We can ask them for their help. They can guard the doorway and make sure we do not steal the body from the tomb." We would have smiled at the absurdity of this happening had the situation not been so tragic.

Because of the pre-dawn dimness it was a little hard to see our way clearly through the gardens of Arimathea to the entombment spot. Suddenly, as we turned onto the curvy path leading to the tomb, we were struck by a blazing light coming from the direction of the tomb. We immediately stopped our soft chatter. Something was very strange! Then we saw a young man clothed in a long white robe. Light seemed to be emanating from him. We women were petrified to the point of hysteria. Then the being—I call him that because I'm sure he wasn't a man—spoke. I'll never forget his words as long as I live. "Be not afraid; you seek Jesus of Nazareth, who was crucified. He is not here; He is risen! Come see the empty place where He once lay." We hesitantly peeked into the bowels of the tomb. It was empty! The angelic being—I'm sure he was an angel—continued, "Now go tell His disciples that He goes to Galilee. There you shall see Him."

The other two women turned in the direction of Mary's home, but I was too shaken to go with them. I excused myself and said I'd catch up with them shortly. As I sat down in the lovely garden, my body shook from head to toe. What had happened to my Lord? The disciples came shortly, but they didn't notice me in the pre-dawn hours. It was evident that they did not believe until they pushed their way into the empty tomb. They came out looking dumbfounded. There was silence as they headed back into town.

After they had gone I walked back to the tomb. I couldn't stop the tears. What had they done with the body? Hadn't they done enough already? My anguished soul shed bitter tears. Suddenly there was a tremendous blaze of light, brighter by far than the noonday sun. As my eyes focused into the light I saw two white-robed angels—there was no doubt in my mind they were angels—one at the head, one at the foot where Jesus had lain. One quietly asked, "Woman, why are you weeping?" When I caught my breath, I choked out, "They have taken away my Lord, and I don't know where they have put Him."

With great sobs that I could not control, I turned to leave the tomb. To my right there stood a man who I supposed was the gardener. When he asked, "Woman, why do you weep? " I quickly realized that the gardener would know about the body being removed. So I knelt and pleaded, "Sir, if you have removed Him, please tell me where you have laid Him, and I will see to it that He is buried properly." The man slowly turned and faced me. "Mary!"

I knew that voice better than I knew my own. Sobbing, I bowed my head to the ground in front of Him. "Master!" was all I could say. I started to reach out and touch Him, but He stepped back slightly. "Don't touch Me, Mary, for I have not yet ascended to My Father. Go, tell the others that I will now ascend to My Father, who is also your Father, My God, who is also Your God!"

I caught up with the two women, and we spread the Lord's message to everyone we saw. Some believed us; some thought we were grief-crazed and had imagined the whole scenario. However, within the next forty days, hundreds of people witnessed the miraculous resurrection of our Lord and became believers.

In fact, just today at least 500 believers were gathered here on the Mount of Olives to see and hear more of what the resurrected Messiah had to say. Hope had been restored, faith renewed, as Jesus made Himself known. We felt like brand-new beings again. Our minds were charged up as we remembered and *understood* His teachings of the past three years. Jesus spoke so tenderly, and yet so powerfully, to us. "It was written in the Scriptures of old that the Christ must suffer, die and rise again on the third day."

Looking at each of us, He continued, "My job is finished, but yours is just beginning. You are to preach the Good News to all nations, beginning right here in Jerusalem. You are to preach repentance and remission of sins, using My name. As you have been witnesses of all that has happened, you must tell it to anyone who will listen. Just remember, the promise that My Father gave is nearly at hand. Tarry in Jerusalem until you are endued with power from on High!"

With that command and commission He lifted His hands in blessing over the entire crowd. Suddenly His feet left the ground and He was carried up into the clouds as we stood and watched in amazement.

"Tarry until you are endued with power." Whatever does He mean? Could that be the Comforter, the Paraclete, about whom He has spoken so many times during these past three years? I remember He told us that this Comforter could not come so long as He (Jesus) was on earth, but that when He returned to His Father, He would send this Comforter, who would teach us and train us and be our guide in all things. Oh, how long do you suppose we will have to wait? And how will we know?

*Mary*
the mother
of *Jesus*

# CHAPTER 12

# *Mary,*

## *Mother of Jesus*

My name is Mary, daughter of Heli of Jerusalem. Some of you might know me better as Mary, wife of Joseph of the house of David. Others will be more familiar with the term "the Virgin Mary." None of the names is important, except to allow you to know more about me and my family.

I feel that a meaningful part of my life has just ended after these past several weeks. Fifty-three days, to be exact. Ten days ago my Son returned to His heavenly Father. There is no grave, though He was entombed in one for three days. There was no graveside service the first time—circumstances did not permit it—and it certainly isn't necessary this time because He isn't dead. That is the remarkable confession on everyone's lips: "He's alive! He is risen! He has ascended to the right hand of G-d!* He is coming again to receive us unto Himself as He promised in His teachings these past several months."

A crowd of about 500 of us watched as He ascended into and beyond the clouds a few days ago. You might ask, "If your son is gone, why are you not grieving? Where are your mourning clothes? What kind of a mother are you to rejoice at your son's disappearance? And what do you mean he didn't die but ascended to G-d? We have all learned that every good Jew goes to the bosom of Abraham at the close of his life on earth. Have you gone mad in your grief?"

Allow me to tell you my unique story from its beginning so you will better understand how my Son has changed the course of human history in a short lifetime. This story could change your life—it has mine.

I was born in Jerusalem, the center of Jewish history for centuries. However, at a young age, my father, Heli, moved our family up north to Nazareth in lower Galilee. It was there that, in the tradition of Jewish culture, I became betrothed to Joseph ben Jacob, a well-known carpenter. He was much older than I, but kind and sincere. My parents felt he would be a good

---

* The name of God was so holy and so revered that the orthodox Jews of Bible times would not write His name in its complete form. So it is today, in the 21st century.

provider and a stabilizing influence in my life. They thought I was too serious for my age, that I needed to socialize more because I was happiest when I was alone. Sometimes it seemed that I could talk to G-d far easier than I could talk to my peers. He seemed to listen anytime, anywhere. I had never heard His voice, but I certainly had felt His Presence in my life.

So it was with great concern that I heard a Voice speak to me one afternoon when I was home alone. Perhaps I was daydreaming—I was not sure—but suddenly a blinding light appeared in the corner of the room. I could barely make out the form of a large being, much bigger than any human. Glistening rivulets of many-colored lights seemed to emanate from his body, as he introduced himself as Gabriel, an angel sent from G-d.

His next words were strange. "Rejoice, highly favored one, the Lord is with you; blessed are you among women!" What kind of a greeting was that? He is a messenger from G-d, and he treats me as if I were a grown woman? Of course, I am betrothed to Joseph, but I am but a young teenager who knows nothing of angels and visions and that sort of thing. If I ever told my parents or Joseph about this, I'm sure they would laugh and call it the vain imagination of a teenage girl.

I was puzzled by all of this until the angel raised his hands protectively over me and said, "Do not fear, Mary, for you have found favor with God." He continued, "Behold, you will conceive in your womb and bring forth a Son, and you shall call His name Jesus."

He paused for an instant, then said, "He will be great, and He will be called the Son of the Highest." He paused as if to allow time for this to sink into my head and my heart. "And the Lord God will give Him the throne of His father David." Another pause. "And He will reign over the house of Jacob forever." Then quietly, but forcefully, he ended with, "And of His Kingdom there will be no end!"

The words seemed to explode all around me: "bring forth a Son." Hopefully, Joseph and I would have many sons, but what did he mean "Son of the Highest"? Everyone knows the Highest is G-d Himself! How could one of our sons be a Son of G-d? "...Give Him the throne of His father David"—all Jews know that our King David was promised an everlasting inheritance, but my son could never be a king. Joseph and I are only slightly above the peasant station in life. We have no royal blood, especially in a country ruled over by cruel Roman military leaders. "...Reign over the house of Jacob"? We are of the tribe of Judah, but reigning would mean a royal role—again, a king. And a kingdom without end? I don't understand. Even if we were of royal blood, we know that many kingdoms have risen and fallen in our nation's history and even in the history of the world. They come and they go. Never are they endless. What did Gabriel mean?

With these thoughts tumbling over each other, all I could force from my trembling lips was, "How can this be?" And then for some reason I quickly added, "...since I have never known a man?" What must

Gabriel think of my bluntness? It didn't come out of my mouth at all like I wanted it to. He must think me a naive, immature girl to say such a foolish thing aloud.

Without hesitation Gabriel answered my question, almost matter-of-factly. "The Holy Spirit will come upon you, and the power of the Highest will over-shadow you. That Holy One who is born will be called the Son of God."

For centuries, since Mother Eve herself and certainly since the beginning of Father Abraham and the Jewish race, every Jewish girl has been told the prophecy of the coming Messiah, Who would be born of a Jewish virgin and free all people from their sins because of His anoint-ing from and relationship to G-d the Father. (The mean-ing of Messiah is *Anointed One*.) The prophet Isaias tells it best in the Holy Writings, as he tells about the coming Messiah:

> For unto us a Child is born, unto us a Son is given; and the government shall be upon His shoulders; and His name shall be called Wonderful Counselor, Mighty God, Ever-lasting Father, Prince of Peace. Of the increase of His government and peace, there will be no end upon the throne of David and over His Kingdom, to order it and establish it with judgment and justice.

"The throne of David"—those are exactly the words Gabriel used. "No end"—again, precisely what

Gabriel had told me. Could it be? Am I the virgin that Isaias prophesied about hundreds of years ago? How can it be? Gabriel told me exactly how it would happen, but it seems impossible!

As if I had spoken these words aloud, Gabriel added more words to what he had already spoken. "Your cousin Elizabeth, the wife of the priest Zacharias, who has been barren throughout her married life, is now pregnant and will bear a son just six months before your miracle Child is born." He looked into my eyes as he concluded, "For with God, all things are possible!" Immediately my heart melted into submission to my Lord as I knelt and proclaimed, "Behold, the handmaiden of the Lord! Let it be to me according to Your word!"

The brightness disappeared as quickly as it had come. I don't know how much time had passed, but I knew something had happened inside me that would change my life forever. And until I was positive that this was not a teenager's dream, I would tell no one—not my mother, and certainly not Joseph!

How would you have reacted to a daughter who came to you with the news that in a few months, before her final wedding vows, she would become the mother of the Son of G-d? If it is a wild dream, no one will ever be the wiser. And someday perhaps I will tell Joseph of my silly schoolgirl dream, and he can shake his head and laugh along with me. But for now I will tell no one.

So it was with great awe that a short time later, when I visited Elizabeth, she greeted me much differently than usual. She was passionate as she welcomed me with, "Blessed are you among women, and blessed is the fruit of your womb." Then it wasn't a dream! But how did Elizabeth know? I could not help but join hands with her, and together we knelt before the Lord as I prayed and sang the song of Hannah:

> My soul magnifies the Lord,
> And my spirit has rejoiced in God my Savior.
> For He has regarded the lowly state of His
>     maidservant!
> Behold, henceforth, all generations
> Shall call me blessed,
> For He Who is mighty has done great things
>     for me,
> And holy is His name!

I stayed with Elizabeth for three months before returning home. My body had confirmed to me that I truly was with child. How would I ever be able to convince my parents of the Source of my condition? And Joseph—would Joseph believe me? I was filled with anxiety and even a little fear as I headed back to Nazareth.

I should have known that when the Lord does something spectacular, He already has put the pieces together to fit the situation perfectly. But He doesn't always do it in an instant. Sometimes a great deal of patience and trust and faith are needed. In this very personal, very private scenario, I felt I should tell Joseph first. After all he was to become my husband, and he had the right to know about the child who he knew was not his.

As I tried to explain exactly what had happened to me three months earlier, I could tell he was trying hard to comprehend what I was saying. But it did not make sense to him, and my Joseph was a logical man. Gently he took my hands in his and looked searchingly into my eyes, as if looking for truth and reality down inside my soul. He did not find it. He proclaimed his love for me, in spite of the situation I found myself in. Both of us were aware of the consequences of my seeming fall. I would be stoned to death in the pit just beyond the city gates. Since Joseph was determined not to allow this to happen, he announced that he would break our betrothal in secret. My life would thus be saved, though I would have to face up to the gossip that was bound to shred my reputation.

I was greatly saddened, but I tried to understand how Joseph was feeling. Any man would react the same way if he were guiltless. Joseph left me, stating that we wouldn't tell my parents until the next day, when we would face them together. I sadly agreed. The angel's words bombarded me: "The Lord is with you; you have found favor in Him; you are most blessed of all women!" I must hang on to those words, whether or not anyone believes me. I am not guilty of the sin that will soon be evidenced in my changing body. Perhaps no one will ever believe me again, but I must trust in the Lord. He is the One who really controls my life, and He knows the truth. I said the words over and over, but I did not feel their confidence and power throughout that night. I fell asleep fitfully, thinking about Queen Esther of old and her proclamation, "If I die, I die!"

Long before sunrise the next morning Joseph appeared at our front door. My heart sank. Why was he so eager to get this over with? My poor parents will be heartbroken. I wished the daylight had never come. Joseph seemed excited as he called me and my parents together, apologizing for his early intrusion. Quickly he related my story to my parents, who sat in doubt and disbelief. Then he told of his decision to secretly break our betrothal. He stopped and smiled shyly. "That will not be necessary now. You see, as I lay down on my sleeping mat last night, I began to dream. An angel of the Lord appeared to me, saying, 'Joseph, do not be afraid to take Mary as your wife. What is conceived in her is of the Holy Spirit!' I knew it was more than a dream; it was the Lord Himself speaking through the same angel who had visited Mary three months ago!

He continued to tell me that Mary will bring forth a Son whom we should name Jesus, which means 'Savior.' The angel said this child would someday save our people from their sins! He said all of this was done in fulfillment of the prophet Isaias' writings: 'Behold, a virgin shall be with Child and bear a Son, and they shall call His name Immanuel, G-d with us!' Our people have spoken of this for hundreds of years. Now our very own Mary has become the chosen vessel of the Lord to bring it to fruition. Blessed be His Name!" And with that Joseph placed his large hands over mine and exploded into a big smile.

My mother and father looked first at us, then at each other. Slowly their expressions changed from embarrassment to doubt to questioning to belief and understanding. They drew me to them, exclaiming, "After all these centuries, G-d has chosen our family to birth and nurture the Messiah, for Whom we have waited so long! What an honor! What a great responsibility!" All four of us lifted our hands and our hearts in praise to Almighty G-d! We immediately celebrated our wedding, but true to the Word of God, Joseph did not touch me until after the purification rites following the birth of Jesus.

His birth was another experience. I was in my ninth month of pregnancy when the decree was sent to Nazareth that Caesar was demanding that a census be taken throughout his empire. Each family was commanded to return to the city of their lineage to register the entire family. Since Bethlehem was the city of David, our ancestor, that was our immediate destination. We hoped we would be back in Nazareth before our Son was born. The prophetic Scriptures of Micah had completely slipped our minds: "But you, Bethlehem Ephrata, though you are little among the thousands of Judah, out of you shall come forth to Me the One to be Ruler in Israel." Without being aware of it at the time, we were fitting into the puzzle that the Lord had begun eons before.

It was a two-week trip from Nazareth to Bethlehem. Although it was tiring the first ten days on the road passed quickly. As was expected the closer we drew to Bethlehem, the more crowded the road became. And then my greatest fear became reality. The lower backache could no longer be excused as the result of the long, bumpy mule ride. It began to deepen and intensify, and by the time we reached the gates of Bethlehem, we knew the birth would never wait until we returned to Nazareth.

It was dark when we reached the inner city where the inns were located. The contractions were coming hard and fast, as Joseph stopped at one inn after another to find us a room. Bethlehem was packed beyond capacity due to the census. I could no longer keep my painful moans to myself; we had to find someplace quickly, or my baby would be born in the middle of the roadway.

Joseph returned to us after having tried the last inn in town. He looked weary, frightened, helpless. "Mary," he said flatly, "There is no room anywhere in this town for us. However, when I told him how desperate we were, the manager of this inn told me about a cave behind his inn where we could at least be in out of the chilly night air. There is fresh straw, and he said he would provide us with a small lantern. That's all he can do." At that point I would have been willing to lie down anywhere. So we trudged our way to the rear of the inn and cleared away a small area where the cattle had been housed. The innkeeper's wife brought us a pitcher of water, along with a lantern.

The next few hours are somewhat of a daze in my memory, but I do remember the relief when the baby was born into the hands of Joseph, and the horrible pain was over. I roused enough to wash the baby and wrap him in swaddling cloths, which we had brought with us, while Joseph cleaned up the entire birthing area.

We had just settled in for the rest of the night, with the baby Jesus lying in a manger that Joseph had filled with sweet-smelling hay, when a group of young shepherds came to the doorway of the cave. At first I thought they probably were looking for a warm place to stay, but I knew they would never leave their sheep alone on the hillside outside the city.

A quick glance around the room suddenly stopped as their eyes fixed upon the manger holding our tiny son. Then they looked at each other in amazement as if to say, "See, it's true! The young men apologized and excitedly began talking all at once. Joseph gently but firmly quieted them, holding his forefinger up to his lips. "Shhh, our baby is newly born and needs to sleep."

They settled down apologetically, and one of the shepherds began to slowly tell us an unusual story. He said they were out on the hillside above Bethlehem guarding their sheep just as they did every night. However, this night was different. They were preparing to roll up in a blanket around the blazing campfire—in fact, a couple of the younger ones were already asleep—when the entire sky lit up as if it were noontime. In the midst of the blazing light stood an angelic being, standing straight and tall, arms outstretched. He paused for a second before speaking. They were so frightened they fell immediately to the ground, their hearts beating wildly. "What is happening?" they wondered. "What is the meaning of what we cannot deny that we see?"

One of the shepherd lads continued, "Our chests continued to thump as the being stepped forward and in a gentle but deeply resonant voice proclaimed, 'Do not be afraid, for I bring you good news, joyous news, which I now tell you but will soon be heard by all people everywhere. On this night, in the city of David, a Savior has been born. He is Christ the Lord, the anointed One sent from G-d! And so you will know that what I say is true, you will find the newborn, wrapped in swaddling cloths, lying in a manger.'

"Swaddling cloths—we wondered, why would a baby be wrapped in grave strips? And why would he be in a feed box where animals eat their hay? As these questions swirled through our heads, there suddenly appeared hundreds, maybe thousands, of angels around the proclamation angel, and the music that filled the night air was like nothing we had ever heard! With uplifted arms the heavenly chorus sang, 'Glory to God in the highest, and on earth, peace and goodwill to all men!'"

Joseph and I looked at each other in astonishment. We knew the shepherds were speaking the truth. And we knew G-d had led them to this place. I shall never forget that moment as the shepherds knelt before the manger and worshiped our Son! Even as they finished, they left us, glorifying and praising G-d for what they had experienced this night. We felt such peace and blessing as we thanked them for coming and confirming what we already knew in our hearts.

Eight days later we presented our baby to the Temple priests in Jerusalem, where He was circumcised according to Jewish law and officially given the name Jesus.

It was while we were at the Temple that another event took place that I shall never forget. An aged man named Simeon was in the Temple at the same time we were. He told us later that he had been told by the Holy Spirit of G-d that he would not die before he had seen the Messiah. Without hesitation he came to us and took Jesus in his arms. Then, lifting his eyes to heaven, he prayed, "Lord, thank You. Now I can go in peace because my eyes have seen Your salvation through this Child, a light to bring revelation to the Gentiles as well as Your people of Israel." Simeon then blessed us as a family and further prophesied: "This Child is destined for the fall and rising of many in Israel. However, a sword shall pierce your own soul, that the thoughts of many hearts may be revealed."

Oh, yes, our Son was going to cause people to make a decision about what they do and do not believe! I wasn't sure what the "piercing" meant, but I knew G-d would give me the stamina I needed, as He had throughout this entire pregnancy and birthing experience. As if that weren't enough of a confirmation, something else happened while we were in the Temple. An old woman named Anna, probably in her 90s, prophesied that our Jesus was to be the redemption of all people. I would cherish forever the words from these wise servants of the Lord!

We were just getting settled in our new temporary home in Bethlehem when we received a visit from foreigners dressed in royal garb. After introducing themselves as Magi from the East, they told us an alarming tale. Almost two years before, after studying the stars for years, they discovered a new star, brighter than any

*134*

they had ever seen. Upon further study, they found that this particular star was the fulfillment of a promise centuries old of the birth of a king who would one day rule the world. If they followed this star, it would lead them to the newborn king. And so, after many months of caravan travel from the East, they found the star resting over our house. After discovering our small boy Jesus, they laid precious gifts of gold, frankincense and myrrh before Him, and fell down and worshiped Him. What an honor that the Lord should so bless us with another confirmation of His Son's birth into the world! I knew I would treasure these moments for the rest of my life.

The Magi had stopped in Jerusalem before coming to Bethlehem. They had approached King Herod asking about the newborn king. The minute they told us this we became frightened because we knew Herod was a wicked man who would accept no other person as his successor, let alone a tiny babe!

It was so. Soon after the Magi left us to return to their homes (they went another route, so as to avoid telling Herod the exact location of Jesus), soldiers entered Bethlehem and viciously killed all male babies less than 2 years old. Herod was going to make certain that any possible future king would never reach that stage in his life—and he knew the king about which the Magi spoke was less than 2.

To show how G-d was protecting us and His Son, He spoke to Joseph in a dream just days before the slaughter. "Arise," the angel of the Lord told him. "Take the young Child and His mother and flee to Egypt. Stay there until I bring you word that it is safe to return, for Herod seeks the young Child to destroy Him." Later we learned in re-reading the Scriptures that the prophet Hosea had foretold this event when he said, "Out of Egypt I called My Son." We stayed in Egypt until Herod's death; then we returned to Nazareth when Jesus was still a small child.

Jesus' growing-up years were non-descript. He was a sober, serious child at times, but He was also fun-loving and humorous. Above all He was obedient—which could not be said of His younger siblings. His meekness empowered Him; His love for everyone caused Him to be popular and well-liked by His peers. I tried not to think about His maturing into manhood and the certainty of His becoming a king of not only the Jewish race but over the entire Roman world. In the meantime, He worked alongside Joseph and became well-known as "the carpenter of Nazareth" after His father's death.

Then came the day that I had known for years would come. At 30 years old, Jesus bade goodbye to His childhood home to go out and "be about His Father's business." His days of ministry had come, and in my heart I knew this was the beginning of the end.

For some time I heard of His whereabouts through the news that began to spread rapidly about His unique ministry. I was told of His baptism at the Jordan River by His cousin John, known as "the Baptist." Those who witnessed the event spoke of the heavens opening and an ethereal dove alighting on Jesus, as a Voice cried out, "This is my beloved Son, in Whom I am well-pleased." Jehovah Himself was announcing to the world that Jesus was the Son of G-d!

Even though I began to fear the political and religious consequences His brothers and I became His closest followers. My responsibility for being His intercessor became important to me. I knew the religious leaders would not stand for what they termed "blasphemy." I knew the politicians would never allow a "rabble-rouser" who could possibly stir the people into revolt against Rome. Jesus preached the Kingdom of G-d and the Kingdom of heaven, and both parties set out to destroy Him. My heart ached because I knew deep down what the outcome was going to be. I didn't want to believe it when Jesus taught on His soon-coming death. I really didn't understand why the perfect Son of G-d would have to die. Nor did I understand His words to His followers about His being raised after three days.

It was the beginning of the third Passover after Jesus had begun His public ministry when everything came to a head. Just five days before the Passover celebration, Jesus was ushered into Jerusalem on a donkey by a crowd of enthusiastic followers. The entire city was aware of Him as the crowd shouted, "Hosanna, blessed is He who comes in the name of the Lord!" As they shouted, they waved palm branches and bowed before Him, honoring Him as they would a king. Although I was proud of Him, my heart was heavy because I knew this could come to no good end. I wanted to protect

Him, but I was helpless. All I could do was pray that Jehovah would keep Him, even as His purpose in life was fulfilled. A 33-year-old should not have to bear such heavy responsibility for the world. If only I could do something!

Immediately after the Hosanna celebration, the atmosphere in Jerusalem changed. The air became heavy with expectancy and evil! By the time Thursday came, the Passover celebration was conducted in every Jewish home, but with a foreboding heaviness. Jesus had told me of His plans to share Passover with His twelve disciples. As He set out toward Mount Zion, where His Passover meal was to be eaten, He bade me goodbye with a kiss that I knew would be His last. How did I know? A mother knows such things, and Jehovah had been speaking to my mother's heart for weeks, in what I now know was preparation.

John, the "beloved" disciple, later told me what happened that night after the Passover meal. In fact, before the meal was completed, Jesus excused Judas Iscariot, who ran from the room as if he were being chased by demons. That is exactly what happened. Judas proceeded to the religious authorities, telling them exactly where Jesus planned to be that evening after the meal. Then he offered to take them to the Garden on the Mount of Olives, called Gethsemane, where he would point out Jesus. For thirty pieces of silver, the cost of an ordinary slave, he was willing to sell His Lord—and lose his soul. Later it was said that after realizing what he had done, he tried to return the money, but was refused. Then he threw down the money in front of the priests, ran out to the Hinnon Valley and hanged himself. Many times in that three-year-period of teaching, Jesus had warned about this temptation. His words, "You cannot serve both God and money" rang so true.

The death march had begun. Jesus was taken to the house of Caiaphas the High Priest, and there He was imprisoned. Throughout the night He was shuffled between the Sanhedrin (who could not legally hold such covert meetings), Pilate the Procurator and Herod the Galilean tetrarch. No one wanted to take responsibility for His death. Finally, Pilate presented Him to the mob for their verdict. Prodded by the religious leaders, they screamed out for His death by crucifixion. Our own people shouted, "Let His blood be on us and on our children!" My own thoughts were, "Dear G-d, do they know what they are saying? What will happen to our race as a result of these prophetic words? I fear we are doomed by our own lips."

And so my Son—G-d's Son—was cruelly flogged beyond recognition and forced to carry His own cross to the horrible hillside outside the city called Golgotha, the place of the skull. Most of the disciples had fled in fear. However, John walked with me, holding me firmly as we trod down that awful path to death.

I don't remember much of the next three hours. As the huge nails were driven into His hands and feet, I felt that my heart was being nailed right along with Him. I vaguely recall His asking the Father to forgive His murderers because they didn't realize what they were doing. As John led me closer to the foot of the cross, Jesus looked down upon us with such pain—and such love—in His eyes. Painfully focusing, first on John, then on me, He said, "John, from now on, she is to be treated as your mother; Mother, this is your son."

I could not contain myself any longer. As John led me back away from the cross, I could hear Jesus gasping as He whispered in anguish, "Into Your hands, Father, I commit My Spirit." And then His final three words, "It is finished!" And with that My Son breathed His last breath, and it was all over. At that moment the sky grew as dark as night, and the wind began to blow fiercely. At the same instant the earth shook so hard and so long that graves opened up and billowy beings floated out and headed into the city.

It was only a short time before the beginning of Passover Sabbath. Physically, I was unable to cope with what I knew would be the next step. G-d bless both Joseph of Arimathea and Nicodemus for having the foresight to carry through that next step. They asked for and received permission to remove Jesus' body from the cross. Hurriedly, they prepared temporary swaddling cloths—the kind in which I had wrapped the Infant Jesus at the time of His birth—and they gently laid Him in the brand new tomb of Joseph, located in a garden just a few feet from Golgotha. The tomb was sealed by the Roman soldiers, and guards were stationed to make sure the body was not removed by His followers.

The Passover days were long and silent. Grief hung in the air, and confusion filled our city. What now?

Why did G-d tell me long ago that my Son—His Son—was to save the world from its sin? What had gone wrong? What did I not understand? What should we have done differently? I had no answers; I only knew that my Son was dead! Passover was finally over, and Mary Magdalene, Joanna and Mary (James' mother) had planned to give Jesus a proper burial. I was in no condition to join them, but they promised to stop by after they had finished.

The sun had barely risen on that first day of the new week when there was a loud clatter at my door. Three wide-eyed women begged to come into the house. Seating me in a nearby chair, they looked at each other and then at me. What was their problem? Why did they look so befuddled and yet so alive with joy? As she drew a deep breath to help compose herself, Mary Magdalene spoke. "Mary, dear, we went to the tomb where Jesus was laid three days ago." She glanced at the other two women for reassurance that she was not dreaming. "Mary, we went to the tomb, and the stone to its opening had been rolled away. I saw it myself. And, Mary, I saw Him; I saw Jesus, alive and well! Now we know what He meant when He said He would be crucified and on the third day be raised again!"

My first thought was that these women had gone insane with grief. My Son was dead. I had watched as He breathed His last breath I knew He had been entombed in Joseph's garden. He was dead!

At that point it was as if my mind opened up wide, and I began to recall the many instances when Jesus had mentioned why He had been sent to earth. The lamb that we had killed last week for Passover was a symbol. Our sins were forgiven for one day, and only one day. When John called Him "the Lamb of G-d Who takes away the sins of the world," we didn't understand. But now it's so simple, so clear. Jesus, as the perfect Lamb of G-d, was sacrificed so that any and all who believe in Him and follow Him will never die but will have eternal life in heaven. My Son died, but He arose from the dead, just as He promised. Now I understand.

But that's not all. In the forty days that followed, Jesus met with hundreds of His followers and continued to teach them, both in Jerusalem and the Galilee. My mother's heart knew that His time on earth was short. He had completed His mission on earth, but His heavenly mission was about to begin—or, should I say, "continue" where He was before He was conceived in my womb?

Jesus and His followers had retreated to His favorite spot on the Mount of Olives when He gave this command to them: "Do not leave Jerusalem, but wait for the gift My Father promised, of which you have heard Me speak. John baptized with water, but in a few days you will be baptized with the Holy Spirit. You will receive power when the Holy Spirit comes upon you, and you will be My witnesses in Jerusalem, in all Judea, in Samaria and to the ends of the earth!"

As we were meditating on what He had said, suddenly His nail-scarred feet left the ground where He was standing, and He slowly floated skyward toward the clouds. It was as if the clouds opened their arms expectantly, and He became enveloped in their embrace. Then He was gone!

Why did He have to leave us again? And who is this Holy Spirit that He spoke about? About this time two men dressed in white robes suddenly appeared on the spot of ground Jesus had just left. "Men of Galilee," they said in unison, "why do you stand here looking into the sky? This same Jesus who has been taken from you into heaven will come back in the same way you have seen Him leave."

These were not mere men; they had to be angelic beings. After all we had been through, this was more than our minds could fully absorb. Slowly and dazedly, the entire group crossed the Kidron Valley and shuffled into the upper room where the Passover, His last supper, had taken place. We knew we had to stay there and wait, although we had no idea for how long.

Day after day went by, and little by little the people left and went back to their homes. We did not—we could not—leave. We must wait, as Jesus had commanded us. How long? Who knows? Our time was filled with singing, worshiping and praying. We were preparing ourselves for something; what it was, we did not know nor did we understand. We only knew we must be obedient.

It was time for us to celebrate the Feast of Pentecost, that holy day that came 50 days after Passover, as set aside by Father Moses. We had dwindled to 120 believers in the upper room. We had begun the day in the usual way, with singing and worship, when an unusual peace and quiet settled upon us. We felt so at unity with one another, our minds in one accord, awaiting the promise of the Father.

Suddenly, the silence was broken. A sound like a violent wind filled the room where we had gathered. Following that were tongues of fire that separated and fell upon each of us. A baptism of love exploded within us, and we found ourselves praising G-d as we had never been able to do in the past. The amazing thing was that we were each speaking in a different tongue, not Aramaic that we had spoken all our lives. This was new; this was different; this was supernatural!

We knew beyond a shadow of a doubt that this was the gift of the Holy Spirit from the Father, just as Jesus had promised us ten days earlier. We felt empowered as never before! Now we knew why we had been commanded to wait until the gift was sent. Now we knew what Jesus had meant when He said, "You will be My witnesses." We knew that we were being sent on a mission, where His message eventually would reach the world. We were ready and willing to follow wherever His Holy Spirit would lead.

We, His followers, will gladly be obedient to His call. When the news is known to all, what will Rome say and do? What will our religious leaders say and do? I haven't a clue, but I do know this: He is the Son of G-d. He came to earth to minister to all who would believe in Him. He has forgiven every sin I ever committed. And I will follow Him for the rest of my life, after which time I will spend eternity with Him in

heaven. My Son was dead; now He is alive! Glory to
G-d in the highest, and on earth, peace and good will
to all men!

I said at the beginning that a certain part of my life
had ended. I was given the honor of bearing the Son of
the Most High G-d! I was allowed to love and nurture
Him for a short period of time; He completed His work
on earth in a short 33 years. Now He has returned to
His heavenly realm, and I know that I shall rule and
reign with Him some day. This is His promise to every
believer! In the meantime, I have work yet to accomplish here on earth before my life is ended, or He
appears in the clouds again, as He promised:

> In My Father's house are many mansions;
> If it were not so, I would not have told you!
> I go to prepare a place for you —
> And if I go to prepare a place for you,
> I will come again and receive you unto Myself,
> That where I am, there you may be also!

Maranatha! Selah!

## To contact Rose Belcher:

Email: rosebelc@juno.com
Fax: (909) 927-3651